Get into R
Sara Kirkham

For USA order enquiries:
Blacklick, OH 43004-0545, USA. Telephone: 1-800-722-4726. Fax: 1-614-755-5645.

For Canada order enquiries: please contact McGraw-Hill Ryerson Ltd, 300 Water St,
Whitby, Ontario L1N 9B6, Canada. Telephone: 905 430 5000. Fax: 905 430 5020.

Long renowned as the authoritative source for self-guided learning – with more than
50 million copies sold worldwide – the Teach Yourself series includes over 500 titles in the
fields of languages, crafts, hobbies, business, computing and education.

British Library Cataloguing in Publication Data: a catalogue record for this title is available
from the British Library.

Library of Congress Catalog Card Number: on file.

First published in UK 2008 by Hodder Education, part of Hachette UK, 338 Euston Road,
London NW1 3BH.

First published in US 2008 by Contemporary Books, a division of the McGraw-Hill
Companies, 1 Prudential Plaza, 130 East Randolf Street, Chicago, IL 60601 USA.

This edition published 2010.

Previously published as *Teach Yourself Running*

The *Teach Yourself* name is a registered trade mark of Hodder Headline.

Copyright © 2008, 2010 Sara Kirkham

Typeset by MPS Limited, A Macmillan Company.

Printed in Great Britain for Hodder Education, an Hachette UK Company, 338 Euston Road,
London NW1 3BH, by CPI Cox & Wyman, Reading, Berkshire RG1 8EX.

The publisher has used its best endeavours to ensure that the URLs for external websites
referred to in this book are correct and active at the time of going to press. However, the
publisher and the author have no responsibility for the websites and can make no guarantee
that a site will remain live or that the content will remain relevant, decent or appropriate.

Hachette UK's policy is to use papers that are natural, renewable and recyclable products and
made from wood grown in sustainable forests. The logging and manufacturing processes are
expected to conform to the environmental regulations of the country of origin.

Impression number   10 9 8 7 6 5 4 3 2 1
Year   2014 2013 2012 2011 2010

Contents

	Meet the author	viii
	Only got a minute?	x
	Only got five minutes?	xii
1	**Why run?**	1
	The physiological benefits	2
	A healthy heart	2
	Better breathing	4
	Increased bone density	4
	Stronger joints and muscles	5
	Higher metabolism	6
	Enhanced energy and improved sleep	7
	Psychological benefits	7
	The runner's high	8
	A workout for the mind	9
	Faster results in less time	10
2	**Getting kitted out**	14
	Buying the right running shoes	15
	Running kit	18
	Running in all seasons	19
	Other running accessories	22
	Ready to get going?	27
3	**Planning for success**	29
	How often should you run?	29
	How fast should you run?	30
	Being running fit	32
	The first few runs	33
	Sample programmes for beginners, novice runners and intermediates	35
	Fitting a run into your day	41
	Scheduling runs into your week	45
	Where to run	48
	Creating a menu of runs	57
	Recording your runs	59

4	**Get set and go – from warm-up to cool-down**	**64**
	Warming up	65
	Footfall and running gait	71
	Breathing tips	73
	Cooling down	74
	Stretches	75
	Rehydrate and refuel	83
5	**Exercise psychology**	**85**
	Dissociation	86
	Running to music	88
	Running with others	88
	How to enjoy your running	93
	Building a running habit	95
	Setting SMART goals	101
	Splitting larger goals into building blocks	105
	Staying motivated with your running habit	108
6	**Food and drink on the run**	**111**
	The basics – carbohydrates, proteins and fats	112
	Nutrition for running	117
	The glycaemic index	118
	Energy for your run	121
	Adjusting your diet to suit your runs	124
	Keeping a food diary and exercise log	128
	Optimum hydration	129
	Sports drinks	131
	Deciding your energy and fluid requirements	133
	Perfect post-run nutrition	135
	Carbohydrate loading	137
7	**Running to suit you**	**144**
	Progressing your running	145
	Creating a menu of runs	146
	Adapting your runs	153
	Heart rate training	157
	Different running methods – Pose and Chi	160
	Burnout and boredom	166
	Non-running cross-training options	168
	What type of runner are you?	171

8 Overcoming obstacles   **174**
   Common running ailments   175
   Sports massage   184
   Running injuries   186
   Things that cause running injuries   188
   Common running injuries   189
   Preventing running injuries   207
   Does my condition prevent me from running?   212
   Asthma   212
   Hay fever   213
   Pregnancy – during and after   215
   Excess body weight   219
   Heart disease   224
   Diabetes   225
   Osteoarthritis   227
   Osteoporosis   228
9 Training for an event   **231**
   Choosing a running event   232
   What to do next   232
   Running programmes for a 5-km run   235
   Running programme for a 10-km run   242
   Seven-day eating plan for 10-km training   247
   Running programme for a half marathon   250
   Carb loading pre-race   257
   Race day   262
   The next step... running a marathon?   265
   Taking it further   **267**
   Index   **271**

Meet the author

Welcome to *Get into Running*!

This book will get you started, helping you to take pleasure in your running and build up an enjoyable, long-term and injury-free running habit. Over the past 20 years I've known hundreds, possibly thousands of people begin an exercise regime. However, whilst running is one of the most common types of exercise to try, it's also quite frequent for beginners to stop during the early days. 'Not enough time', 'too difficult', 'found it boring' or 'picked up an injury' are common reasons cited.

One of the problems with running is that we're almost too familiar with it – we know what running is, so that's what we set out to do... run. The thing is, if you haven't run for a long time, maybe since you were at school, you can't expect your body to be able to cope without a 'running in' period. *Get into Running* eases you into the running habit – helping you to fit short, easy runs into your lifestyle, starting you off at a level that's achievable and enjoyable, enabling you to gradually build up running fitness and achieve the goals you have set yourself. Running too far or too quickly too soon will feel uncomfortable, and is likely to put you off for life! Your first few runs should actually be 'jogs' or 'walk-runs'. You wouldn't expect to begin with an advanced class in any other type of exercise, so why should running be any different?

This book is not written by an elite runner, but by someone who enjoys running and who understands that sometimes it can be difficult. I know from personal experience that it can be hard to motivate yourself to go out running; that it can be tough to keep going when it feels like too much effort; that it can be demotivating when you don't seem to be getting anywhere. So I understand how you might feel, and I have put everything I can think of to help you into this book – information to help motivate you to go running;

dissociation tricks to help get you through your run when you're finding it difficult or boring; sports nutrition tips to energize you; and ideas for different types of runs to keep things interesting. You might be thinking, 'If running's *that* tough, why would I want to do it?' Maybe because running is one of the most effective types of exercise there is, capable of bringing enhanced health to every cell in your body, and promoting such intense feelings of well-being that the 'runner's high' has become a well-known expression.

This book is packed with practical advice, hints and tips to keep you going, along with invaluable insights from both a professional and personal point of view. There are plenty of tools to help you through the tougher parts of a regular and effective exercise regime, but also ideas to help you vary and enrich that routine, with a variety of runs, training programmes and running gadgets. But what I hope you'll really take away from this book is the way that you begin to feel – not just whilst you're out running but also in between runs.

Get into Running will show you how to get started, how to keep going, and how to be the first one over that finish line!

Sara Kirkham, 2010

Only got a minute?

You can choose no better way to exercise, keep fit or lose weight than running. Even swimming and cycling take second place to running as far as calorie expenditure is concerned. In fact, research has also shown that fat utilization is up to 28 per cent higher during running than cycling. So, if you're looking for a type of exercise that is probably the most effective, and the least time-consuming, you've found it!

What's more, there are so many additional benefits to be gained from regular running, it's no surprise it is one of the most popular choices of exercise. Regular running has been proven to:

✓ lower blood pressure
✓ lower cholesterol levels
✓ reduce heart rate
✓ improve lung function
✓ reduce body-fat levels
✓ improve fitness levels
✓ strengthen bones.

... and these are just a few of the benefits. The advantages of regular running encompass body size and shape, fitness levels, disease prevention and mood enhancement. If you've ever seen someone running in the cold or the rain and wondered why, the answer lies in the way running makes you feel. The sensation of moving your body through the air, across the ground at speed, feeling all your limbs working together in unison can be truely exhilarating.

Getting started is simple – all you need is a pair of trainers and somewhere to run! *Get into Running* is the perfect guide both to get you started with your running regime and to keep you motivated. You'll find out what kit you need, how far and fast you should aim to run, what to wear, what to eat and how to stay injury-free. There is a wealth of practical tips that will make your running easier and even more enjoyable than it already is, as well as a variety of running programmes that range from 'pre-run walking programmes' to those enabling you to compete in a half-marathon. So what are you waiting for?

5 Only got five minutes?

The fact that you are reading this suggests you are looking for something … maybe a new hobby, a way to get fit or lose weight… or just something to make you feel better within yourself. There is certainly a link between regular exercise and well-being, and research has proven that this association peaks when we walk or run between 11 to 19 miles per week. This may sound like a lot, but you'll soon be able to run or walk-run three or four miles, and doing this three times a week not only places you in this 'enhanced well-being zone' but also achieves the activity levels that doctors recommend for physical health. Who knows, you might even experience that fabled runner's high! One thing is for sure: you are guaranteed to feel better, fitter, younger and stronger if you take up running.

Running is probably the most adaptable type of exercise there is, so there's no excuse not to try it! You can fit a run into your day at a time that suits you – first thing in the morning to get your day off to a flying start, at lunchtime to boost energy levels through the afternoon, or after work to provide a great transition between your job and home. Just think – no expensive health club memberships or equipment to pay for, no specialist kit or classes required… just you, a pair of trainers and a spare half-hour! What could be easier? As you get fitter you can easily adapt your runs to create new training effects: simply choose a longer route or incorporate some sprints or uphill sections into your run. Equally, if you have less time available, you can make your running route shorter and just run it in a faster time – running is that adaptable. There's no partner required as in racquet sports, no opening times or class timetables to work around, and, if you're working away or staying with friends, you don't have to put your exercise sessions on hold – that is, of course, as long as you've remembered to pack your running kit!

Whether you need help to get started or specific specialist advice, you will find the information you want in *Get into Running*. Discover what running kit is essential and which gadgets are really useful; improve your fitness with goal-setting tips and information on different types of running; and follow the eating plans to fuel your running. If you need extra motivation to keep going, Chapter 5 'Exercise psychology' is guaranteed to help, with useful tips on dissociation and how to create a running habit. It isn't running that can cause injury, it's the *way* that we run, so Chapter 7 'Running to suit you' introduces different running styles that might help you to avoid common running ailments such as shin splints or knee injuries, whilst Chapter 8 'Overcoming obstacles' covers common causes of running injuries, how to spot them and treat them, and, most importantly, how to avoid them.

Using this book, you'll be able to create a running regime that suits you, with help planning your runs into your week, deciding where to run, how long to run for, and what type of run to do. And whenever you feel the need for extra motivation or professional advice, or want to change your running programme, a quick look at the index will guide you to specific topics from gait analysis and carbohydrate loading to entering a running event.

It is amazing how running can transform you – from feeling utterly exhausted to feeling totally energized. You will soon become addicted to the elevated mood and higher energy levels that running generates. All you've got to do is pull on those trainers and get out there!

1

Why run?

In this chapter you will learn:
- *the health benefits of regular running*
- *how to achieve the runner's high*
- *why running is the best calorie burner.*

There are so many benefits to be gained from regular running, it's no surprise it's one of the most popular choices of exercise. It is probably the easiest form of exercise to begin – all you need is a pair of trainers and somewhere to run! Although there are enough running gadgets and accessories to keep the most ardent enthusiast entertained, you don't need any specialist kit apart from a decent pair of running shoes, which makes running one of the most affordable and accessible types of exercise you can do.

Although some people may find it difficult (and therefore less enjoyable) to begin with, and others find it challenging to stick to a regular running schedule, the benefits of running far outweigh any obstacles you might put in the way. This chapter explores those benefits, whilst subsequent chapters offer help and advice to get you started... and keep you going.

The physiological benefits

There are many physiological benefits to be gained from regular running, including reduced risk of coronary heart disease, stroke, obesity and diabetes, osteoporosis, Alzheimer's disease and some types of cancer. The American College of Sports Medicine is an authority on the effects and benefits of exercise. Their recommendation for all healthy adults is as follows:

▶ *Do aerobic exercise three to five days per week comprising activity that uses large muscle groups and can be maintained continuously.*
▶ *Exercise at between 55 per cent and 90 per cent of your maximum heart rate.*
▶ *Exercise for 20–60 minutes.*

Going out for a run meets all three recommendations and also ticks all of the boxes for achieving the health benefits listed below:

✓ *lower blood pressure*
✓ *reduced resting pulse*
✓ *reduced cholesterol levels*
✓ *improved cardiovascular efficiency*
✓ *stronger bones and reduced risk of osteoporosis*
✓ *strengthened connective tissue and joints, reducing the risk of injury*
✓ *higher energy consumption, resulting in lower body fat levels and reduced body weight*
✓ *reduced risk of insulin resistance – diabetes and metabolic syndrome.*

A healthy heart

First and foremost, your cardiovascular fitness is set to improve with every run, jog or power-walk that you do. A European study ('Hypertension in Master Endurance Athletes', *Journal of*

Hypertension, Nov 1998, M. Hernelahti et al.) evaluated the effect of regular running on blood pressure in middle-aged men. Blood pressure was significantly lower in the runners than in those who did no exercise.

Regular running reduces the risk of coronary heart disease (CHD) through a number of factors:

▶ *improved health and function of the heart and arteries*
▶ *reduced body fat (high body fat is a risk factor for CHD)*
▶ *reduced blood pressure (hypertension is a risk factor for CHD)*
▶ *reduced cholesterol levels (elevated total or 'bad' LDL [low-density lipoprotein] cholesterol is a risk factor for CHD).*

Insight

One study (*Archives of Internal Medicine*, Williams 1997) showed up to a 50-per-cent reduction in high blood pressure in long-distance runners compared with non-runners. However, you don't have to be an endurance athlete to gain benefits: the amount of 'good' cholesterol in runners has been found to increase in line with every extra kilometre run. Having a high level of HDL ('good') cholesterol helps to lower the 'bad' LDL cholesterol, which is linked with increased risk of atherosclerosis and heart disease.

LOWER PULSE RATE

Whenever we exercise, our heart has to pump more blood in each stroke to deliver nutrients and oxygen to the rest of the body. Doing regular exercise, such as running, simultaneously provides exercise for your heart – and the more often it is put under pressure to pump more blood around the body, the better it becomes at doing it.

With regular running, the heart chambers become larger and are able to accommodate a larger volume of blood. This increases the amount of blood the heart can pump in one heartbeat. Obviously, the more blood that can be pumped around the body in one beat, the fewer times per minute the heart has to pump, which reduces your pulse at rest and during exercise.

MEASURING YOUR PULSE

A 'normal' resting pulse is approximately 72 beats per minute, although this tends to increase with age or with declining health. If you are new to regular running and are interested in the difference it will make to your cardiovascular health, take your resting pulse now and check it once a month to see if it decreases. Find your pulse by placing your fingers on the inside of your wrist, just down from your thumb. Once you've found your pulse, count the number of beats over one minute and note it down. As well as having a lower resting pulse, measuring how long it takes to return to your resting pulse after your run is a good way to measure your improving recovery rate.

Better breathing

Your aerobic capacity is the ability to take in and use oxygen. The increased air consumption that occurs during running trains our lungs in the same way that it trains the muscles in our legs. As with anything, if we repeat something habitually or make greater demands on our body, we achieve a training effect and experience an improvement in function. Thus, lung and respiratory function are improved through running.

Increased bone density

Running is a weight-bearing exercise and, as such, it requires our skeleton to bear our body weight. Bone strength, or bone mineral density, is determined by several different factors, but new bone tissue is only laid down if it is needed – in other words, if you don't use it, you lose it!

Osteoporosis is a condition in which bones have become porous and brittle due to a reduction in new bone cells and lack of mineralization; if bones are not regularly 'taxed', they gradually become weaker. Regular running promotes the laying down of new bone cells and minerals, making bones stronger, particularly the weight-bearing bones in the feet, ankles, legs and hips, which are often bones liable to fracture upon a fall.

Insight

Regular runners have significantly higher bone mineral density, especially in the heels, legs, pelvis, and lower spine. However, bone mineral density in upper-body bones has also been found to be slightly higher in runners.

Stronger joints and muscles

In addition to stronger bones, regular running creates stronger joints, muscles, tendons and ligaments in the lower half of the body through increased use, and an enhanced supply of blood and nutrients. Ligaments are straps of connective tissue that attach bone to bone and strengthen joints; tendons are the connective tissue attaching muscle to bone.

Having stronger joints, tendons and ligaments will contribute to problem-free running and better everyday function. Strong tendons help to prevent muscle strains and strong ligaments prevent sprains. If you slip on ice or go over on your ankle, having stronger muscles, tendons and ligaments in the lower parts of your body will help to prevent a groin strain or a sprained ankle when the muscle or joint is put under stress.

Increased muscular strength has a number of additional benefits:

▶ *more strength for everyday activities and other sports*
▶ *improved muscular balance, reducing the risk of injuries*

- *improved posture as muscles become more balanced*
- *increased metabolism – more lean tissue (muscle) uses up more energy*
- *improved body image as you feel and look more toned, fit and healthy.*

Higher metabolism

Without building large muscles, regular running will enhance the amount of lean tissue you have, and this increases your metabolic rate. Your metabolic rate determines the number of calories you use up during every hour of the day, whether you are running, sitting or sleeping; a higher metabolism uses up more calories and makes weight management much easier.

REDUCED LEVELS OF BODY FAT

As a weight-bearing exercise of reasonably high intensity that uses large muscles, running uses up more calories per hour than most other activities. Check out the table below for a comparison, though bear in mind the number of calories used will differ depending on body weight, percentage of lean tissue and speed.

Activity	Approximate calories per hour (kcal)
Running	640
Aerobics	400
Rowing	400
Swimming	320
Cycling	240
Walking	210

Information from www.brianmac.co.uk

All these activities have their merits, but where calorie consumption is concerned, running is a winner!

Enhanced energy and improved sleep

It's amazing how a run can transform you from feeling completely exhausted and lethargic to feeling completely energized. Even though going out for a run may sometimes be the last thing you feel like doing, you'll quickly learn how much better you feel afterwards, and become addicted to the elevated mood and higher energy levels. As your heart, lungs and tissues become more adept at transporting and using nutrients for energy, and more oxygen is pumped around the body with improved circulation, energy levels increase. Stronger, more efficient muscles, better glucose control and weight loss also contribute to higher energy levels and make everyday tasks easier to do.

Regular exercise such as running can promote sleep and enhance deep sleep, leaving you feeling more rested in the morning. However, you will be more alert for a few hours after a run, so make sure you give yourself time to wind down if you run in the evening!

Psychological benefits

There is a close connection between the mind and the body, and this is heightened whenever we run. Once you find your pace during a run you will experience this – the body feels like it was made to run and you are likely to feel very 'connected' to your body. It has been said that, after a certain time on long runs, the mind takes over for the body. You are unlikely to experience this on every run but when you do you may...

- ▶ *experience enhanced 'flow' in the body, also known as 'chi'*
- ▶ *achieve a personal best time*
- ▶ *experience the runner's high.*

The runner's high

One of the best-known psychological merits of running is the so-called 'runner's high'. If you are already a runner you may have experienced this already – an enhanced, even euphoric, mood that makes you feel on top of the world. Although some runners only experience this 'high' once they have been running for a couple of hours at a fairly fast pace, it is also known that running for just 20 minutes is long enough to relieve anxiety and boost mood.

There are a number of other factors that also contribute to enhanced mood whilst running, increasing the likelihood of a 'runner's high':

- *running outside, particularly in scenic, natural surroundings*
- *running at approximately 75 per cent of your maximum heart rate*
- *finding a comfortable pace that you can relax into*
- *having a good run and experiencing a sense of mastery.*

There have been many theories to explain the 'runner's high', the best known concerning 'feel-good hormones' called endorphins released during and after running. Even short spurts of intense exercise can cause a rush of endorphins, as they are released to reduce stress and pain in the body. However, more recent research suggests that the 'high' is due to other chemicals or neurotransmitters that are also released during exercise.

There are many theories about the runner's high, with conflicting opinions about which chemicals actually cause this elevation in mood, how far and how fast you have to run, and whether the 'high' is due to exercise or successful completion of a challenge. However, one thing is for sure: whether you experience euphoria after running a marathon, or become addicted to the enhanced mood you feel after your 30-minute beach run, stick with running and you will experience your own 'runner's high' at some point!

A workout for the mind

An unexpected psychological bonus of running is the enhanced clarity of mind that enables you to work through problems, enjoy enhanced creativity or simply 'clear your mind'. You may think that you don't have time to exercise, but when you return from a run you are likely to experience all of the following:

- ✓ *a boost in creativity*
- ✓ *a clear, focused mind*
- ✓ *a plethora of fresh ideas*
- ✓ *greater productivity.*

So, taking time out for a quick run can actually make you more productive and save you time in the long run!

You might find that during a run you switch off from work and 'the daily grind', or you may find yourself easily sorting out work problems, planning a study schedule in your head, or finally being able to come to a decision about something that's been worrying you for weeks. One thing is for sure: you will certainly benefit psychologically as well as physiologically from running.

Regular running has been repeatedly associated with reduced anxiety and stress, lower incidence of depression, improved mood and enhanced self-confidence. In a large-scale study (5,451 men and 1,277 women) published in the journal of *Medicine and Science in Sports and Exercise* in 2006, it was concluded that increases in exercise such as running, jogging or walking were associated with greater emotional well-being and fewer symptoms of depression. This research showed that the association between regular exercise and well-being peaked when individuals were running, jogging or walking between 11 and 19 miles per week.

Several studies have illustrated that regular running reduces stress, lifts mood and decreases the risk of depression and diseases such as Alzheimer's. These positive effects are due to a number of factors including increased blood flow carrying oxygen and nutrients to the brain during and immediately after exercise, and the increased release of 'feel-good' endorphins.

INCREASED SELF-ESTEEM

Improved self-esteem stems from a number of changes that occur following any regular exercise routine:

▶ *You feel better about your body due to the changes that have taken place (weight loss, improved body shape, toned muscles).*
▶ *Levels of several neurotransmitters and endorphins are elevated through regular exercise – these hormones and chemicals enhance feelings of relaxation and contentment.*
▶ *Regular exercise generates a feeling of accomplishment.*
▶ *Exercise also creates a positive feeling that you are doing something good for yourself: this enhances self-esteem and confidence levels.*

Faster results in less time

As well as the health and fitness benefits that running provides, it also offers key advantages over other types of exercise.

QUICKER RESULTS

Running produces results quicker than most types of exercise. It takes less time to achieve fitness, health or weight loss goals for the following reasons:

▶ *Running is a fairly high-intensity activity, which means that you will see fitness benefits sooner than you would from easier types of exercise.*
▶ *As a weight-bearing exercise, running uses a higher number of calories than non-weight-bearing activities such as rowing, cycling or swimming done at the same level of intensity and for an equal length of time.*
▶ *In addition, because running uses some of the largest muscles in the body (the legs and gluteal – bottom – muscles), this also creates a higher caloric expenditure, making running number one as far as weight loss and body-fat reduction is concerned.*

Insight

The net calorie expenditure (the energy you use up after deducting calories that would have been used regardless of activity) during a run is twice the amount used in walking the same distance. Research has also shown that fat utilization is up to 28 per cent higher during running than during cycling.

TIME EFFICIENCY

Lack of time is one of the main reasons we give for not exercising, yet running has to be the easiest type of exercise to fit into a busy day – all you need is a 30-minute window!

▶ *If you can run from home or work, your exercise session begins straightaway, rather than sitting in traffic to get to the gym.*
▶ *You can adapt your run to suit the time you have – if you have to work late or something crops up, just do a shorter run. A high-intensity sprint will provide different training benefits to a slower, longer jog, and the diversity creates a more interesting training programme.*

▶ *You can run at a time to suit you – you don't have to work around class timetables or health club opening hours, and you won't suffer when activities are cancelled. Anytime, anywhere, you can go out for a run.*

▶ *Although running with others is a great option, you don't need a partner to go running with.*

ADAPTABILITY

▶ *You can choose to run with others or on your own.*

▶ *You can run wherever you are – working away from home, on holiday, staying with friends…*

▶ *You can adapt your run to suit the way you are feeling, with shorter runs accommodating tiredness or lack of time, and longer runs making the most of the time available.*

THINGS TO REMEMBER

▶ *Running will give you quicker results in less time than almost any other type of exercise.*

▶ *It requires no training, no specialized kit or equipment.*

▶ *You can do it at any time, anywhere, for as long as you like.*

▶ *It uses up more calories than walking, swimming, cycling and most other forms of exercise – see the calorie comparisons in this chapter!*

▶ *As a weight-bearing exercise, it can reduce the risk of osteoporosis.*

▶ *As a cardio-respiratory exercise, it improves the health of the heart, the lungs and the cardiovascular system.*

▶ *Because running is a higher-intensity form of exercise, it stimulates endorphin release, lifting mood and reducing stress.*

▶ *You not only use up more calories whilst you are running, but your metabolic rate increases, enabling you to use up more energy between runs as well.*

▶ *Running is something you can choose to do alone or with friends, inside or outside, competitively or at your own pace.*

▶ *It doesn't cost anything!*

So with all these benefits, what are you waiting for? Pull on your trainers and get out there!

2

....

Getting kitted out

In this chapter you will learn:
- *how to choose the right type of running shoe*
- *how gadgets can help you to plan your run and record the results*
- *how listening to music can help your running.*

The only two things you need to start running are a reasonable pair of running shoes or trainers, and somewhere to run. Simple! Of course, there are a number of other things that will contribute to an enjoyable, safe and effective run – all of which are covered in this chapter – but the essentials are you, your running shoes and a running route.

This chapter discusses the plethora of running kit and running gadgets that can make your running more comfortable and enjoyable, and may even improve your running technique and ability. If you are new to running, you may need tips on how to buy your first pair of running shoes, and if you are returning to running, you might find a gadget such as a heart rate monitor or an iPod just the thing to keep you motivated.

One thing's for sure, if you get the 'running bug', you'll gradually accumulate running kit and accessories as you clock up the miles! Read on to discover what the world of running has in store for you.

Buying the right running shoes

Whereas the average pair of trainers may seem adequate for a run, a pair of running shoes (trainers specifically for running) will provide a better fit and function for running. Running is a high-impact activity because you have only one foot on the ground at any one time. This greatly increases the force with which your foot hits the ground (two to three times your body weight), particularly at speed, so a certain amount of shock absorption is necessary for injury-free running.

Running shoes provide support in the mid-sole, and cushioning around the heel and underneath the forefoot. This is why a pair of plimsolls or squash shoes, for example, are not suitable for running – these shoes just don't have adequate cushioning for the impact of running.

Many trainers have an air, gel or foam cushion within the structure of the shoe that you can sometimes see, but running shoes will usually be clearly marked as such in any sports shop.

If you can, visit a specialist running shop where the assistants will advise you on the best running shoe for you, based upon your footfall and how much running you are doing, as well as your price range! Out of all the things you might purchase to feed your running habit, your running shoes should take priority – a good pair can put a significant amount of extra speed and bounce into your stride, and many new personal-best times are achieved with a new pair of trainers! You may not realize how 'tired' your old running shoes are until you run in a new pair.

TIPS FOR YOUR PURCHASE

▶ *Go to a specialist running shop for the best advice – the assistants are also more likely to be runners themselves.*
▶ *Good fit is everything – be prepared to choose shoes that are a better fit over another pair in your favorite colour!*

- *Don't presume you will always need the same size in a running shoe – the size you need may alter depending upon the make of running shoe.*
- *You may be advised to try a pair of shoes a half-size larger than your normal shoe size. This is because the foot tends to travel forwards in your shoe as your feet hit the ground; damaged nails and nail beds are common among runners, so make sure there is space between your toes and the front of the shoe. You should be able to wiggle your toes and have approximately half an inch space at the end of your toes.*
- *Many people have one foot slightly bigger than the other – buy the size of running shoe that fits your bigger foot – you can always wear an extra sock on the other foot!*
- *Try your running shoe on with a pair of socks that you usually run in for the best fit. If you have running socks, don't forget to take them with you.*
- *Feet do get warmer later in the day or after walking around or working out – this is a better time to ensure a well-fitting shoe, rather than when your feet are colder and slightly smaller.*
- *A new pair of running shoes should feel comfortable straightaway without a 'running in' period. If you can feel any part of the shoe rubbing against your foot, this is likely to cause a blister – try a different shoe.*
- *Be prepared to move around in the running shoes and even have a little jog up and down in the shop if possible. If it's a specialist running shop they'll probably expect you to want to do this anyway.*

Insight

If you find a pair of running shoes that really suit you, buy a second pair! Companies change the design of their running shoes all the time, and you might find it difficult to find shoes to suit you next time. You can keep the second pair for when you need them, alternate between both pairs to double their life expectancy, or wear the second pair every now and then when you feel you need a boost or want to set a personal best!

MATCHING SHOES TO FEET

The shape of your foot and the way that you run (your running 'gait') will determine the best type of running shoe for you. In a typical heel–toe footfall, the heel lands first (heel strike), followed by the middle of the foot as the arch of the foot flattens to absorb impact; then the front of the foot contacts with the floor and pushes off for the next stride. This creates a 'rolling action' from heel to toe, and from the outside of the foot to the centre. However, footfall differs from one person to the next:

▶ *We all place different amounts of pressure on different parts of the foot when we walk or run.*
▶ *Some people land on one side of the heel and don't 'roll in' enough (a likely sign of this is that your shoes will wear out on the outside of your heel).*
▶ *Some people have less of an arch in the foot and are known as being 'flat-footed'.*
▶ *Others 'roll in', or pronate, too much, which can put the lower legs, knees and even the hips out of alignment.*

The assistants in a specialist running shop should be able to help you find the right pair of running shoes, and may be able to decipher your footfall by one or more of these means:

▶ *looking at where your existing shoes or trainers are worn*
▶ *assessing your running gait*
▶ *using a foot scan facility (a pressure-sensitive mat that captures your 'footprint' with digital imaging as you land on it).*

Insight

Always tie your shoelaces in a double knot to stop them coming undone, and keep toenails as short as possible to avoid them banging into the front of your trainer and becoming damaged.

Running kit

Other than a good pair of running shoes, you could 'get by' with
most types of workout kit, but if you are running several times
a week you'll soon discover the benefits of wearing kit made
specifically for running. Comfort is the main thing to consider when
running. You need to be warm enough but not too hot in winter,
and cool but still protected from the sun in summer. You should
not be aware of anything you are wearing – bottoms that constantly
need pulling up, shorts that chaff, tops that ride up or make you
sweat. Clothes like this will make your run unenjoyable and prevent
you from focusing on your running technique and form.

BOTTOMS

▶ *Shorts should be comfortable and allow for a full running
stride – if they are made from a material that doesn't 'give' or
are not made for running, you could find your shorts cutting
into your thigh every time you lift your leg up.*
▶ *You might favour 'cycle' shorts or shorter running shorts with built-
in COOLMAX briefs in the men's shorts, which remove the need
for a jockstrap. Look for specialist material such as Dri-FIT that
will keep you dry. Pockets for small keys or money may be useful.*
▶ *Bottoms such as Ronhill tracksters can be worn for running in
winter. Try to avoid heavy sweat bottoms or baggy trousers,
which are too cumbersome and will create 'drag', especially
if you're running against the wind. Again, zipped or hidden
pockets can be useful.*
▶ *Bottoms with some reflective material in the design are useful
for running in the dark or in poor weather conditions. Don't
make the mistake of running in all dark clothing – motorists
won't see you until the last second.*

TOPS

▶ *An essential item for women is a running bra or top with
built-in support. Apart from being uncomfortable, lack of
support can cause the ligaments that support the breast tissue*

to be overstretched, and this is irreversible. Workout crop tops often have a hidden support layer inside, but this won't be as effective as a proper running bra or running crop top.

▸ Most vest tops, T-shirts or long-sleeved running or workout tops are adequate for running, although all of these are available as specific running apparel, made from material to help keep you dry, with reflective strips etc.

▸ Running jackets are a good investment for winter running. They are lightweight, usually showerproof and wind resistant, giving you some protection from the weather without getting you overheated during your run. The extra layer of clothing also helps to keep you warm. Running jackets will normally have some sort of reflective material or strips on them, which is especially important if your running kit is dark in colour.

SOCKS

Although you can easily run in normal sports socks, you're bound to come across specialist running socks and wonder what running socks have that normal socks don't.

▸ Ideally socks should not be made of cotton, as cotton does not take sweat away and may lead to blisters. Specialist running socks are made of material that will take away moisture from the skin and help to keep feet dry, with thinner material or ventilation panels across the top of the sock to allow the foot to breathe.

▸ Running socks often have a reinforced heel and forefoot to help reduce impact to the foot and offer a little extra support.

▸ Good running socks are seamless to avoid rubbing, and should be a snug fit to avoid material wrinkling.

▸ Running socks may have a right and left sock to give a better fit and provide support and cushioning exactly where it's needed on each foot.

Running in all seasons

If you're hooked on running, you'll be going out no matter what. You may find that you won't begin a run if it's pouring down,

but if you're already out... well, you may as well finish your run!
There's something quite refreshing about running in the rain, and
you should find light drizzle and showers no problem at all. During
winter months you do need an extra layer, although you'll find
that you warm up five minutes into your run, so don't be put off
running when it's cold – a clear, frosty day can be one of the nicest
types of weather to run in.

RUNNING IN COLD WEATHER

- *A long-sleeved running top and a running jacket with long-legged trachsters or running bottoms should keep you warm enough.*
- *You lose a lot of heat through the head, so wearing a hat helps to reduce this in really cold weather. If you find that you 'overheat' when you run and find wearing a hat uncomfortable, a headband to keep wind and cold off the ears can be an invaluable investment.*
- *If you suffer with earache in cold or windy weather, invest in a headband rather than a hat to cover the ears.*
- *Icy weather gets to the fingers, so a thin pair of gloves is also useful, although you may find you want to take them off halfway through your run once you're warm, so pockets may be useful.*

RUNNING IN HOT WEATHER

- *You should wear sunscreen if you're running in sunny weather – an hour's run is like an hour's sunbathing. If you would normally wear sunscreen whilst out in the sun for an hour, you also need to apply it for your run – use a sport or waterproof variety, otherwise it'll come off as you begin to sweat.*
- *A peaked cap can help to keep the sun off your face and out of your eyes; a visor may be better (unless you have a tendency to burn your head), as it shades the face and allows heat to escape through the head. Running caps are typically made from lightweight material that will take away sweat and have*

mesh panels for added ventilation; they often have a longer peak to shade the whole face and may have a flap to protect the back of the neck from the sun.

▶ *Some runners favour running in sunglasses (again, you can get sports shades specifically for running) to avoid glare from the sun.*

▶ *Look for running clothes made from a man-made fabric that takes sweat away from the body as it forms, preventing you from feeling sweaty and clothes feeling damp.*

The other thing to consider during hot weather is whether you need a water bottle to take on your run, though this should be essential only if you are running for an hour or more. You'll find lots of information on hydration in Chapter 6 'Food and drink on the run', but here are some tips to help you decide whether you need a water bottle.

▶ *You lose more water throughout the day in hot weather, so you need to drink more to ensure that you are well hydrated before your run.*

▶ *Most runners find it difficult to carry water and drink whilst running.*

▶ *There are a number of fluid vessels available, ranging from small bottles you can easily grasp in your hand, 'bottles' in the shape of a handle so you can grip them, and water containers that you can attach to a belt.*

Insight

Before you rush out and buy a water bottle, consider the following:

▶ *Any water you carry is extra weight.*

▶ *Your body won't rehydrate immediately, so taking water with you on short runs is probably a waste of effort.*

▶ *Good hydration comes from drinking ample fluid in the 48 hours prior to a run, including replenishment of fluid lost during earlier runs, not from drinking during a run.*

Other running accessories

As with any sport or activity, there are many gadgets and accessories for running. Although you can enjoyably run for years with nothing other than a good pair of running shoes (and a running bra for women), you can also go to town on kitting yourself out.

GADGETS TO HELP YOU RECORD AND MONITOR YOUR RUNS

A range of gadgets enable you to measure variables such as how far and how fast you are running, how many calories you are using up, or what your average pace and heart rate are. These gadgets range from simple pedometers to top-of-the-range heart rate monitors.

Pedometers

Pedometers are one of the cheapest and easiest ways to record your runs, although prices vary from a few pounds up to more than £40 for those with more features (or from $7 to $45). If you choose to use a pedometer, make sure you get one suitable for running rather than for walking. You attach the device to your waistband or put it in a pocket – so for running you need to make sure it's secure and not jumping around.

The key function of a pedometer is to count how many steps or strides you have taken, although some will also indicate the following:

- ▶ *distance travelled*
- ▶ *run time*
- ▶ *estimated calorie expenditure*
- ▶ *time of day*
- ▶ *estimated speed.*

Some also have a stopwatch facility and memory.

Some pedometers allow you to download all of this information onto websites, enabling you to log and monitor your progress and achievements. Websites may also offer additional online support such as setting you new running targets each week.

Foot pods

A foot pod attaches to your trainer or running shoe and will measure your distance, time, speed and pace. Foot pods often come as part of the package with more expensive heart rate monitors, but can be purchased individually, usually costing from £50 (or $99).

Although foot pods can be used on their own, they are often used in conjunction with a pedometer or a heart rate monitor, measuring the distance travelled on your runs, and, with some gadgets, sending this information directly to your monitor. You can set it using your own running stride, but many foot pods are now very accurate and don't need to be calibrated. Some foot pods have an 'alarm' to let you know if your speed strays outside the pace you might have set for yourself and will also measure average speed and lap distance.

Heart rate monitors

A heart rate monitor usually includes a chest strap that picks up your heart rate and a watch (monitor) that picks up the information sent from the chest strap. The monitor will record and calculate a wide range of information from each run, such as heart rate, speed, distance and calorie expenditure. This information can be stored in the monitor, or downloaded onto your computer or specific websites. Heart rate monitors vary greatly in price with basic models available at about £30 ($50) and top-of-the-range units for serious athletes and enthusiasts costing several hundred pounds.

Here are some of the common features found on a heart rate monitor:

DURING YOUR RUN

▶ *Speed (pace) is calculated from the distance and time taken. You can set a pace alarm, which warns you when to speed up or slow down.*

▶ *You can measure each lap, mile or kilometre on a run to analyse your pace throughout your run, showing lap time, average heart rate and lap number.*

▶ *Some monitors have heart rate training zones pre-programmed (50 per cent, 60 per cent, 70 per cent, 80 per cent and 90 per cent of maximum heart rate) and you can add your own personal heart rate training zones as well. The monitor bleeps when your heart rate moves from one zone to another, helping you to stay in a particular training zone such as aerobic fitness or 'fat burning'.*

▶ *You can monitor your resting heart rate to give an indication of fitness levels.*

▶ *Calorie expenditure can be measured.*

▶ *Most monitors have a stopwatch facility, which is essential for an accurate start and finish time on any run and also useful when doing interval work or running in a race or event.*

▶ *Throughout your run you can switch between calories used, time, lap time, pace, speed, distance and heart rate.*

See Chapter 7 'Running to suit you' for more information on heart rate training and interval training.

AFTER YOUR RUN

▶ *Most monitors have a memory, and you can either keep your run information stored in your monitor, or download it onto your computer or a website. Seeing your run and heart rate information displayed on a graph can be extremely motivating and makes it much easier to analyse how your running is going.*

▶ *Monitors tend to save information such as date and start time, distance run, speed and pace, calories used, duration of exercise, average heart rate, maximum heart rate and training zone information for each run, as well as additional information such as lap time or intervals if these functions have been used.*

▶ *Some monitors organize run information into weekly totals and overall totals as well as for individual runs.*

MUSICAL MOTIVATION

Many runners listen to music on an iPod, MP3 player or portable radio for motivation or to distract them from their running. This is known as dissociation – see Chapter 5 'Exercise psychology' for more information. There are both benefits and drawbacks to tuning in to music or radio during your run, so it's really a case of personal preference.

Positive aspects of listening to music whilst running

✓ *It takes your mind off exercising.*
✓ *It can provide motivation.*
✓ *You can create a soundtrack to match your run, with specific tracks for a tough hill or a long stretch of road.*

- ✓ It can help you to switch off from your surroundings if your route isn't very interesting or is noisy – a busy road, for example (but see 'warning' below).
- ✓ It will help you to switch off from the gym environment if you're running on a treadmill and want to focus on your run.
- ✓ The right music can relax, motivate or empower you – you can choose your run and your music to suit your mood.
- ✓ The right beat can help you to find your running pace and regulate your breathing.
- ✓ Music can enhance the 'feel-good factor' of exercise.

Warning

However, listening to music on headphones makes you less aware of things going on around you, such as traffic, cyclists or other people, making you more prone to an accident or injury, and more vulnerable to being attacked or assaulted.

Follow these tips for safe running with music:

- ▶ Run safe, familiar and public routes rather than quiet paths.
- ▶ Run with a running partner if they also prefer music to your company!
- ▶ Run with a dog.
- ▶ Buy 'open-air' headphones that allow some outside noise to enter your ears so you can stay partially aware of your surroundings, or just keep the volume low.

ALL-IN-ONES!

Music, motivation, run information, goals and challenges all with one gadget!

For runners who enjoy running to music, Nike has a great running product called the Nike+ iPod Sport Kit. A sensor inserted into your running shoe measures your speed, distance, time and calories used, and wirelessly sends this information to the iPod receiver on your arm. You can set a 'power song' for that difficult hill or long stretch that you always struggle with, and at the touch of a button you can listen to your run time and pace instead of having to look at your receiver or a monitor. You do, however, have to have a pair of Nike+ shoes so that you can insert the sensor underneath the lining.

Once your run is finished, the receiver downloads your run information onto your computer and the Nike website (www.nikeplus.com). This website can turn your running habit into a lifestyle, enhancing your running with a number of tools to:

▶ *record and analyse your run information*
▶ *set yourself new running goals*
▶ *download a wide selection of music perfect for running*
▶ *choose and measure the distance of runs in your area*
▶ *set up running challenges with other Nike+ iPod users.*

_____

Ready to get going?

So, if you've got the essentials covered and don't need tips on route planning or putting your running schedule together, you might want to go for a run right now. If you need an idea of how far or how fast to go, visit the start-up programmes in the next chapter, or if you want some advice on warming up for your run, skip ahead to Chapter 4 'Get set and go – from warm-up to cool-down'.

Once you have a few runs under your belt you might find you need or want additional kit or gadgets to make your runs more comfortable or enjoyable, but for now, if you're kitted out, you're ready to run.

THINGS TO REMEMBER

Here's a quick checklist, in order of priority, to get you started...

- ✓ *running shoes*
- ✓ *running kit (supportive top for women)*
- ✓ *water bottle if needed*
- ✓ *watch*
- ✓ *sports drink or energy gel, if needed*
- ✓ *hat, gloves and extra layer in cold weather; sun lotion/ sun visor/sunglasses in hot weather*
- ✓ *door key if needed!*
- ✓ *gadgets if you use them – for example a heart rate monitor, foot pod or iPod.*

3

Planning for success

In this chapter you will learn:
- *how to set your running pace*
- *how to plan your running routes*
- *how to organize your first six-week running schedule.*

Although you can plan your route, distance and running schedule before you begin running, most runners tend to just go out for a run and take it from there… and that's the great thing about running – no planning required, just do it! However, a little bit of planning can go a long way, so if you're not sure how fast you should run, how far to go or where to run, read on for inspiration, advice and ideas. If you've tried running before but not stuck with it, this chapter will help you to plan for a successful second try.

How often should you run?

This obviously depends upon whether you are new to running or not. If you are returning to running or have already begun, then you probably already have a weekly running routine. All that needs to be said for the novice or intermediate runner is to make sure you allow recovery time between runs. It's easy to become 'addicted' to the enhanced mood that regular running produces, but it's important to have rest days, particularly after longer runs.

If you have a heart rate monitor or can take your pulse, you should ideally wait until your resting heart rate is back to normal before running again. If it's slightly elevated, this is a sign that your body is still recovering from the last run and isn't ready for a run yet, or that you are slightly below par – for example, you may be getting a cold. Remember, this is different to your training heart rate, which obviously returns to normal after exercise. In addition to this, muscles, tendons and ligaments need time to recover and you also want to avoid 'burn out' from too much running.

If you are new to running, always allow recovery time between runs. Running every other day is a great routine to follow, allowing three runs a week, with either an extra run or an extra rest day on alternate weeks. It's important to create a running habit, and, to do this, you need to run at least twice weekly and should really aim for three times a week. Don't worry about running too far or too fast at this stage – it's all about building the habit and making small improvements.

How fast should you run?

It's essential to begin running at a level that is appropriate to you. A very common mistake in new runners is to run too fast. At this stage, you are going out for a jog, not a run, and you'll soon realize that you cannot continue at your fastest running pace for very long! Gasping for breath and having to stop or walk can be demotivating for new runners, but this is where recovery walking comes in. Walking isn't a sin, and recovery walking can be planned into your route and gradually reduced until you can jog for the majority of your run. You will find recovery walking has been included in some of the beginner running programmes in this book.

Your jogging or running speed will increase as you become fitter, but until your fitness improves even low-intensity exercise can cause you to be out of breath. A good way to judge whether you are running at the right level is something called the Talk Test.

Using the Talk Test to set your pace

The Talk Test is used throughout the health and fitness industry to help exercisers measure their exercise intensity level. If you can have a full conversation with someone without getting breathless, you're unlikely to be exercising at a high enough intensity to create a training effect – you're taking it easy! However, you should be able to speak a sentence or two – if you can't say anything, your intensity level is too high to be maintained for long, certainly not throughout an endurance activity such as running. At the right intensity, if you do have a running partner, you should be able to converse a little as you run.

RUNNING PACE

Pace can relate to two things in running – the speed that you run at, and the comfortable running pace that you will slip into on a good run, known as 'finding your pace'. When runners talk about falling into a pace, or finding their pace, they are usually referring to the pace that is their normal, average running speed; a pace that can be maintained for the whole run. Falling into your pace comes when running fitness has improved and your body is more 'comfortable' with the mechanics of running. This often happens when enhanced energy or fitness levels enable better running form (or vice versa) and running suddenly feels effortless. Although this can happen naturally, some runners find that specific running methods help them to achieve this, such as Pose running (see Chapter 7 'Running to suit you' for more information).

You don't need to know your running speed, but fellow runners may ask what pace you run at to assess what 'level' you are at. Speed isn't everything – mileage is just as important – but you will automatically increase your speed (pace) as you become fitter and as your running improves.

Calculating your running pace is simple. You need to know how long a specific run takes you, and how far it is. Your pace is measured in the same unit as your distance – miles or kilometres. You can either put the details of your run into an online pace calculator (an example is included in Taking it further at the end of this book) or calculate it yourself. Alternatively, you can always find out your pace on a treadmill, although this is usually a slightly faster pace than road running. You are likely to have an average pace, but will have a different pace for hill runs, off-road running, treadmill running, etc., as different terrains and inclines all affect your speed.

How to calculate your running pace

A ten-kilometre run that takes one hour to complete would give you a ten-kilometre/hour pace. If your run is less or more than an hour, simply divide the number of minutes it took by the distance run.

For example, if you ran four miles in 40 minutes...

40 minutes divided by four miles = ten minute/mile pace.

If it takes 50 minutes to run four miles, divide 50 by four, and your pace is a 12.5 minute/mile pace.

Being running fit

Each different sport or activity creates its own specific training effects, but even if you already exercise, only some of the training effects will overlap with those you achieve with regular running.

In other words, you may be fit but not running fit. Any different activity that we do is new to our body, and even if you cycle, swim, do aerobics classes or weight-train regularly, you will not be running fit. Even sprinters can find long-distance running difficult and vice versa – this is the law of specificity, which you will use to your advantage when you begin to train for a running event.

Any existing cardiovascular fitness will certainly aid your running efforts, but to be running fit you have to run regularly. Training adaptations in the body are specific to the activity that creates them, so although good cardiovascular fitness will help your running, unless you are exceptionally fit, you are still likely to find your first few runs demanding.

The first few runs

▶ *Novice and intermediate runners are likely to already have a weekly running routine, so your focus is likely to be upon progression and running form. For those brand new to running, or returning after a long break, here are some tips to get you started, together with a sample training programme for your first six weeks. Remember, if you've had a long break from running you won't be able to carry on where you left off – you need to start again. However, you may find that you'll progress quicker than first time around.*

▶ *Don't try to run too fast – maintain a comfortable, steady pace that leaves you able to speak a few sentences if conversing with a running partner.*

▶ *Choose a fairly flat route to begin with.*

▶ *Softer terrain such as footpaths, tracks or grass will enable you to get used to the impact of running before going onto roads or pavements.*

▶ *Choose a route that is no longer than two miles, or plan to run for approximately 20 minutes. Remember that this is likely to include some recovery walking and should begin with a warm-up walk.*

▶ *Make a note of how long your run took you or how long your route was so that you can measure your progress over the next few weeks.*

RECOVERY WALKING

Many runners (experienced and beginners alike) think that walking is not an option. If your idea of running is as black and white as 'I should be running flat out for the entire run, on every run', then you are in for a shock and likely to give up as soon as you begin! There is nothing wrong with slowing your pace or doing a little recovery walking to reduce the intensity enough so that you can continue and finish your run. In the first few weeks it's all about getting out there, completing your runs and getting fitter, and running at a slower but steady pace for 20 minutes is better than intermittent sprints with complete stops.

It's important to realize that doing a little recovery walking can be the key to a long and enjoyable running habit. Recovery walking is not an excuse for a rest, but simply a reduction in intensity for a short period of time. Recovery walking is like power-walking – you must maintain a fast pace, and break into a jog again as soon as you can. Here is a sample training programme to illustrate how this works.

Warm-up with walking	5–10 minutes
Jog (not run!)	1 minute
Recovery walk	2 minutes

Repeat the one-minute jog followed by two minutes' recovery walk five times over, giving you a 20 to 25-minute session including your warm-up walk. Naturally, if you can jog comfortably for more than one minute, just keep going until you need to drop to a recovery walk for two minutes. You should make a mental note of how long you jogged for in each running interval, and aim to improve this as you progress through the next six weeks. A sample programme of progression is shown below.

Sample programmes for beginners, novice runners and intermediates

If you are new to running, or returning after a long break from running, follow the programmes and schedules for beginner runners. If you are already running but still quite new to it, or are returning after a short break, try the novice runner programmes. Existing runners should follow the intermediate programmes and schedules. If you are unsure which category you fit into, find the appropriate starting point for you by finding your current running distance or duration in these programmes.

SIX-WEEK RUNNING PROGRAMME FOR BEGINNER RUNNERS

1 *Complete a five-minute warm-up walk before your first run section.*
2 *Walk less and/or run for longer if you can, progressing to a run with no recovery walking as soon as you are able to do so.*
3 *Alter your training days to suit your week, but try to alternate running days with rest days where possible.*

	MON	TUES	WED	THURS	FRI	SAT	SUN
WEEK 1	Run 1 min Walk 2 min 6 times	Rest day	Run 1 min Walk 2 min 6 times	Rest day	Run 1 min Walk 2 min 6 times	Rest day	Rest day
TIME	18 mins		18 mins		18 mins		
WEEK 2	Run 2 min Walk 2 min 5 times	Rest day	Run 2 min Walk 2 min 5 times	Rest day	Run 2 min Walk 2 min 5 times	Rest day	Rest day
TIME	20 mins		20 mins		20 mins		

(Contd)

	MON	TUES	WED	THURS	FRI	SAT	SUN
WEEK 3	Run 3 min Walk 1 min 5 times	Rest day	Run 3 min Walk 1 min 5 times	Rest day	Run 3 min Walk 1 min 5 times	Rest day	Rest day
TIME	20 mins		20 mins		20 mins		
WEEK 4	Run 4 mins Walk 1 min 4 times	Rest day	Run 5 mins Walk 1 min 3 times	Rest Day	Run 5 mins Walk 1 min 3 times	Rest day	Rest day
TIME	20 mins		18 mins		18 mins		
WEEK 5	Run 6 mins Walk 1 min 3 times	Rest day	Run 7 mins Walk 1 min 3 times	Rest day	Run 8 mins Walk 1 min 2 times	Rest day	Rest Day
TIME	21 mins		24 mins		18 mins		
WEEK 6	Run 10 mins Walk 1 min 2 times	Rest day	Run 11 mins Walk 1 min 2 times	Rest day	Run 12 mins Walk 1 min 2 times	Rest day	Rest Day
TIME	22 mins		24 mins		26 mins		

Remember: Workout times do not include time spent warming up or cooling down.

Top tips for your first run

▶ *Start off with a five-minute walk and break into a gentle jog. Each run should be like moving through the gears in a car, starting off slowly and gradually building up to a cruising speed.*

- ▶ *Don't run too fast – this is a common mistake with anyone new to running. Go at a gentle jogging pace and see how far or how long you can jog for before you become breathless.*
- ▶ *When you can't run or jog anymore, drop to a recovery walk – a fast walk that keeps your heart rate elevated but allows you to get your breath back.*
- ▶ *Carry on alternating jogging with recovery walking as and when you need it for the rest of your run.*
- ▶ *Don't choose a long route until you know how far you can comfortably run and how long it will take you.*

Each week, with regular running, you'll find that your sections of recovery walking (or slower jogging if you are alternating this with running) will become shorter and the runs will become easier.

Rest days
Rest days are there to enable your body to recover from your runs. A complete rest from exercise is known as passive rest, and active rest is when you may do a different type of exercise such as swimming or weight training – different enough to running to still achieve the rest required. If you are keen to improve your fitness levels or lose weight more quickly, you might choose to do different activities from running on your days off. You should, however, still aim to have two passive rest days a week.

Your first run after a rest will tell you if you are completely rested or not. Watch out for symptoms which suggest you are running too frequently:

- ▶ *You feel tired and lack energy during your run.*
- ▶ *The run feels more difficult than usual.*
- ▶ *You take longer to complete the run.*
- ▶ *You develop an injury.*

Any of these can mean that you need more rest between runs, or that you are not eating enough carbohydrates to provide energy for your running. It takes up to 48 hours to replenish glycogen stores (stored carbohydrate in your liver and muscles), and can take several days after a number of longer or more difficult runs. You may experience this feeling towards the end of your running week when you have already completed a number of runs.

Eating more carbohydrates such as porridge, potatoes, rice or pasta may provide the extra energy you need without having to have an extra rest day. Runners often find that the first run after a rest is the best run of the week, so this may be a good day to complete longer or more difficult runs.

SIX-WEEK RUNNING PROGRAMME FOR NOVICE AND RETURNING RUNNERS

If you are new to running but already fit, or are returning to running after a break, you may not need to incorporate recovery walking into your runs. Try this sample plan for your first six weeks' running:

	MON	TUES	WED	THURS	FRI	SAT	SUN
WEEK 1	20-min run	Rest day	20-min run	Rest day	20-min run	Rest day	Rest day
WEEK 2	25-min run	Rest day	25-min run	Rest day	25-min run	Rest day	Rest day
WEEK 3	30-min run	Rest day	30-min run	Rest day	30-min run	Rest day	Rest day
WEEK 4	30-min run	Rest day	30-min run	Rest day	35-min run	Rest day	Rest day
WEEK 5	35-min run	Rest day	35-min run	Rest day	35-min run	Rest day	Rest day
WEEK 6	40-min run	Rest day	40-min run	Rest day	40-min run	Rest day	Rest day

This programme concentrates on increasing running time, building from running for 20 minutes up to 40 minutes over a six-week period.

More than 40 minutes is a good running time to aim for as this improves endurance and creates several cardiovascular training effects, as well as providing a 'fat burning' workout (see Chapter 6 'Food and drink on the run' for information on which fuels we use during different types of run). However, if you haven't got a 40-minute window of time, instead of increasing the run time, aim to either increase your speed or complete more difficult routes as shown below.

Ways to run for the same duration but increase intensity

Lack of time often gets in the way of running or progressing your running. However, there are simple ways of making a run more difficult without running for longer:

- ▶ *You can run uphill.*
- ▶ *You can do some interval training.*

Both of these types of running are discussed in more detail in Chapter 7 'Running to suit you'.

Top tips for increasing intensity

- ▶ *Choosing a hilly route will make you work harder on the uphill sections.*
- ▶ *You can also choose simply to run up a hill and jog slowly back down, repeating this training for the time you have available.*
- ▶ *Interval training involves running at a faster speed for a determined distance or time, then easing off until you get your breath back, then repeating a faster section of running again, continuing this through your run.*

As well as the training effects gained from higher-intensity runs, incorporating different types of run into your running schedule also adds interest. Take a look at the sample six-week running schedule on page 40, which incorporates higher-intensity runs but keeps run duration low.

	MON	TUES	WED	THURS	FRI	SAT	SUN
WEEK 1	20-min run	Rest day	20-min run	Rest day	20-min run	Rest day	20-min run
WEEK 2	Rest day	20-min sprints	Rest day	25-min run	Rest day	Rest day	30-min run
WEEK 3	Rest day	Timed 25-min run	Rest day	20-min sprints	Rest day	Rest day	Do a hill run
WEEK 4	Rest day	Timed 25-min run	Rest day	Do a hill run	Rest day	20-min run	Rest day
WEEK 5	20-min sprints	Rest day	Interval running	Rest day	Timed 25-min run	Rest day	Interval running
WEEK 6	Rest day	Do a hill run	Rest day	Timed 25-min run	Rest day	Interval running	Rest day

Top tips for further increasing intensity

▶ *Go for a faster time on your timed runs.*
▶ *Extend the distance on the hill run each couple of weeks or go for a faster time.*
▶ *Go for a faster lap time on your sprints.*
▶ *Reduce the recovery phases in the interval training runs or increase the pace of the faster intervals.*

SIX-WEEK RUNNING PROGRAMME FOR INTERMEDIATE RUNNERS

As a regular runner you will already have a set running routine and may already be running for longer than 40 minutes. If this is the case, you may find the information on goal setting, dissociation techniques or creating a menu of runs more helpful than a set training plan. However, you may have a specific goal to work towards, such as a running event, and if this is the case you should plan your six-week running programme accordingly. For example, this six-week running programme begins by increasing running time, then incorporates some longer runs with interval training for diversity and different training effects, then culminates with specific 10-km timed runs.

	MON	TUES	WED	THURS	FRI	SAT	SUN
WEEK 1	40-min run	Rest day	40-min run	Rest day	40-min run	Rest day	Rest day
WEEK 2	45-min run	Rest day	45-min interval training	Rest day	50-min run	Rest day	30-min Interval training
WEEK 3	Rest day	50-min timed	Rest day	30-min sprints	Rest day	40-min run	Rest day
WEEK 4	Timed 10-km run	Rest day	30-min sprints	Rest day	40-min interval training	Rest day	Rest day
WEEK 5	Timed 10-km	Rest day	40-min run	Rest day	Rest day	Timed 10-km	Rest day
WEEK 6	Rest day	Timed 10-km	Rest day	Rest day	40-min run	Rest day	Timed 10-km

Fitting a run into your day

You have several options in choosing when to run:

▶ *an early-morning run before breakfast*
▶ *a run in the morning or afternoon if you're at home*
▶ *a lunchtime run if running from work*
▶ *running after work in the evening*
▶ *weekend running.*

Although this may seem fairly obvious, it's worth taking some time to plan when you will run, and organize your day around it. For example, when you run will affect your eating times, fluid intake, whether you need to take your running kit to work with you, whether you need to get up earlier than usual, and so on. In addition, the time you have available during a day affects the distance and intensity of that run.

There are different benefits from running at different times of the day, but the important thing is to just get out there, regardless of whether it's first thing in the morning or during the evening.

Insight

If you are a regular exerciser or runner, you may find that your body has become attuned to exercising at a certain time of the day, and you may find running at different times of the day more difficult. If you are preparing for a race or some other running event, regular running at the time of day this is due to be held will help you.

EARLY-MORNING RUNNING BENEFITS

✓ *Early-morning running means that, regardless of how your day turns out, you have already done your run. This is a good option for those with very busy schedules or unpredictable jobs.*
✓ *New runners who run first thing in the morning are more likely to create a successful running habit.*
✓ *Early-morning running is a great energizer, setting you up in a great frame of mind for the rest of the day.*
✓ *Whilst running on an empty stomach isn't for everyone, an early-morning run can be an effective 'fat burning' workout as you will have less stored carbohydrate available and will use more fat for fuel. (See Chapter 6 'Food and drink on the run' for more nutrition information.)*

Insight

Choose early-morning running if...

▶ *work has a habit of getting in the way of your running schedule*
▶ *you lack motivation and are likely to talk yourself out of a run*
▶ *you tend to feel too tired to run in the evening*
▶ *you want to lose weight.*

LUNCHTIME RUNNING BENEFITS

✓ Research shows that exercise at lunchtime improves focus, concentration and effectiveness during the afternoon when energy and concentration levels usually drop.

✓ A lunchtime run is a great way to socialize with work colleagues, simultaneously increasing the effectiveness of the whole team. Why not organize a lunchtime running club at work? You may be able to offset a longer lunch break by starting work a little earlier or staying a little later.

✓ Running at lunchtime means that you can relax once you've finished work – you don't have to juggle traffic, dinner, family time and fitting a run into your evening.

✓ Planning a run around work can provide a useful schedule for your running habit – for example, Monday-to-Friday lunchtime runs create a serious running schedule of five times a week.

✓ Running at lunchtime gets you out of the workplace, providing a change of scenery and increasing the likelihood of a healthier lunch – you are unlikely to feel like eating a stodgy meal after your run and there is less time left to go to the pub!

✓ Running during the day is easier in poor weather conditions such as ice and snow, or during the winter months when it might be dark before and after work.

Insight

Choose lunchtime running from work if...

▶ you regularly have to work late – a lunchtime run will make you more effective throughout the afternoon, and working late is likely to affect your running plans

▶ you suffer with energy slumps in the afternoon

▶ you have too many things that compete for time during the evening such as family or work commitments, a busy social diary, TV and the sofa...

▶ you have a long or time-consuming drive home that leaves you feeling too tired to run.

EVENING RUNNING BENEFITS

✓ Early evening is the time when our circadian cycle is at it highest, making 4 to 6 p.m. the most effective time for a run.

✓ You are less likely to have pressing work engagements that will limit your run time, so you can relax into your run and extend it if you feel like it.

✓ You can avoid the midday sun by running in the evening during the summer months.

✓ Running after work is an effective way to unwind, switch off and leave the office behind, creating a good transition between work and home time. Working through work issues or 'to do' lists in your head for the next day whilst you run is effective and helps to free your evening from work worries.

Insight

Choose evening runs if…

▶ you are stressed or uptight when you finish work – the run will help to unwind and de-stress you

▶ you have spent all day at a desk, a machine or driving – a run will help to loosen and rebalance muscles and help you to relax during the evening

▶ you struggle to separate work from home life and find it difficult to switch off from thinking about work

▶ you don't have any time during the day!

Of course, there is always the weekend to fit in extra runs as well, and you may find that doing a couple of longer weekend runs forms the backbone of your running schedule, with little or no running from Monday to Friday. Part-time jobs, self-employment, working from home and shift-working all present different opportunities for slotting regular runs into your week – but if you don't plan when you are going to run, you are less likely to do it!

Insight

Our circadian rhythm regulates the way in which our body functions, including things like body temperature, blood pressure, metabolism and hormone levels. We tend to find exercise easier and more productive when our body temperature is at its highest – that is, in late afternoon to early evening. During this period muscles are warm and flexible, blood pressure and resting heart rate are lower, reaction time is quicker and our strength peaks.

Scheduling runs into your week

Running programmes are included throughout this book, but the programmes here focus upon fitting runs into your week, with tips for successfully adjusting to whatever life throws at you!

The following is an example of a planned running schedule:

MON	TUES	WED	THURS	FRI	SAT	SUN
Run after work		Run after work		Run after work		Bonus run
4 miles/ 40 mins		4 miles/ 40 mins		4 miles/ 40 mins		4 miles/ 40 mins

This running plan may involve one or more routes all of the same distance or time. If you are new to running you might begin with a smaller distance, and should concentrate on either distance or running time rather than on speed. For example, based on the training programme above you would plan to either:

▶ *run for a distance of 4 miles three or four times a week, or*
▶ *run for 40 minutes three or four times weekly.*

Plan to complete three or four runs weekly. Planning a 'bonus run' means that on a good week you'll do an extra run, and if you miss a run during the week, the bonus run becomes a more essential part of your weekly schedule.

FITTING RUNS INTO A BUSY SCHEDULE

It's a common mistake to forgo a run completely just because you haven't got the time it normally takes to run your usual route. If this continues for long, your running habit will soon reduce to occasional runs, and all the benefits of regular running, including progression, training effects and running ease, will soon disappear, making the running that you do seem less enjoyable and increasing the likelihood of your running habit disappearing.

If you are regularly missing your runs, you need to plan how to fit running into your week in a different way. For example, three runs of four miles in the evening could be adjusted as follows to provide the same mileage.

MON	TUES	WED	THURS	FRI	SAT	SUN
				Long run		Long run
				6 miles/ 60 mins		6 miles/ 60 mins

Or...

MON	TUES	WED	THURS	FRI	SAT	SUN
Run 2 miles before work & 2 miles after work		Run 2 miles before work & 2 miles after work		Run 2 miles before work & 2 miles after work		Bonus run
4 miles/ 40 mins		4 miles/ 40 mins		4 miles/ 40 mins		4 miles/ 40 mins

If you have set yourself a running goal, it's also worth planning to run a little more, as this gives you room to accommodate the odd run that may not happen. For example, if your running goal was to complete 500 minutes of running over the next six weeks, your new schedule could look like this:

MON	TUES	WED	THURS	FRI	SAT	SUN
Run before work		Run before work		Run before work		Bonus Run
2 miles/ 20 mins		2 miles/ 20 mins		2 miles/ 20 mins		6 miles/ 60 mins

Shorter two-mile or 20-minute runs are easier to complete before work, and with a longer bonus run every other weekend, you would complete 540 minutes of running over six weeks by following this schedule.

So, if you are struggling to find time for your usual run, try to do one of the following instead:

▶ *Check your normal route on a map to see if there are any short cuts enabling you to shorten your run.*
▶ *You can always run to a certain point on your route and back again, fitting your run to the time available.*
▶ *If you have less time to run, choose a more difficult route (include hills, for example) or run faster – this will increase the intensity of your run and still provide a training effect. Running faster means that you can cut less distance from your normal route as you'll be completing it in a faster time.*
▶ *Go to a local field/playground/track and do some sprints for however long you have available – you can stop the training session whenever you need to without having to worry about getting home within a specific time, and sprint training provides effects that you might not be getting from your usual runs.*

▶ *Cut your run into two! You may not have your usual hour available (for example), but you may be able to do two shorter runs – for example, one before work and a second run after work. Although this is less convenient, if you are set on completing a certain distance or clocking up running time, this enables you to achieve your goal.*

▶ *Increase the distance or running time at the weekend or during the following week to compensate if this is viable.*

▶ *Think of other time slots during the day that you wouldn't normally consider – could you get up an hour early to fit in an early-morning run, or fit in a run at lunchtime?*

Insight

It's important to remember that your run doesn't have to be a specific distance or duration to be effective – just because you have a one-hour-long running route doesn't mean that a running slot of 40, 30 or even 20 minutes can't be useful. In a busy lifestyle you have to make the best use of the time you have, and if this means fitting runs into half-hour slots through the week, then that will form your running programme. Shorter runs can be as effective as longer runs if the route and intensity level are adapted accordingly, enabling you to make the most of the time you have.

Where to run

The most important factors, particularly if you are new to running, are to choose a route (or routes) that are easy to get to and enjoyable to run – you might choose a local path or track in the woods, have a great run along the seafront, or decide to run around the block. Any run that you can do from your front door is the best option, though your run will be greatly enhanced if you are able to run in natural surroundings – the feeling of being at one with nature can be a contributing factor to the 'runner's high'.

The route you choose will depend upon the following variables:

▶ *how long you want to run for*
▶ *what distance you want to run*
▶ *what sort of terrain you want to run on*
▶ *where you are running from (home, work etc.)*
▶ *whether you prefer to run straight from home or drive to another running location.*

ROUTE LENGTH

As a guide, if you have never run before or are not engaged in any regular exercise, you should choose a route of one or two miles to begin with. To measure the distance, you can drive the route as suggested below, use a map, or you can plot your run on a website such as www.nikeplus. You may not be able to run the whole distance, and that's fine – you'll be using the run/walk training option outlined earlier in this chapter. As you get fitter or whenever you have more time available, look for options to lengthen your route as follows:

▶ *Run the route twice.*
▶ *Extend your route by adding a 'there-and-back' sprint at an appropriate section of the run.*
▶ *Add on an extra block or loop to your run route.*

Insight
Driving round the block in the car is a simple way to find out the distance of a local running route. Once you find your pace, you'll be able to estimate the distance of off-road runs based upon your run time.

For returning runners
If you have already done some running, it is likely you have a route or two and will know what sort of distance you can run. However, do remember that if you've not run for a while, you need to reduce the distance, time or intensity of your run, as you will have lost some of the training benefits you enjoyed as a regular runner.

Training effects decline in approximately one-third of the time they took to achieve, once regular training (running, in this case) has stopped. For example, the benefits of running three times a week may take ten weeks to achieve, but will be lost due to de-training in approximately three weeks.

The following factors affect the intensity of your first few returning runs:

▶ *The shorter the time since you stopped running regularly, the lower the de-training effect.*
▶ *The more time your running habit spanned over, i.e. if you ran for a couple of years as opposed to a few weeks, the more likely you are to be able to return to running at a higher level.*

In addition to distance there are a number of other things to consider when planning your running routes – would you prefer to be road running, trail/cross-country running, running on a beach or running on a treadmill? Or maybe a combination of these would suit you best?

ROAD RUNNING

Whether you are in a city or out in the country, the most likely running you'll do is road running (although you will mostly be running on the pavement rather than the road). The differences between running actually on the road or on the pavement are as follows:

▶ *It is safer running on the pavement rather than the road.*
▶ *Most roads are asphalt (tarmac) and pavements are often concrete; tarmac creates less impact on the bones and joints during a run.*
▶ *Roads often have a slope or camber at the sides that can affect your running gait and cause injuries.*

Road running (either alongside or on a road) is easier than off-road routes in many ways, although there are also drawbacks to consider.

Benefits of road running

- ✓ *Road running is easily accessible to most people – just step outside of your front door and run around the block or down the lane – you have a ready-made route.*
- ✓ *It's easy to plan a road run from a local map, and if you can drive the route, you know exactly how far you are running and can accurately calculate your running pace.*
- ✓ *The terrain is likely to remain the same (i.e. concrete or tarmac), so you don't have to adjust your running form or speed on different running surfaces. This enables you to relax into a comfortable running speed and find your 'pace'.*
- ✓ *Most roads are likely to be lit by street lights during winter months, and busy roads may enable a sole female runner to feel comfortable to continue with winter running in the evenings.*
- ✓ *Roads and pavements still allow for running after periods of wet weather (try running through fields after days of rain!), making this type of running a year-round option.*

Drawbacks of road running

- ▶ *If you live in an area that is busy with traffic, the noise and air pollution can lessen the enjoyment of your run. Wherever possible, try to plan your runs along roads with the least amount of traffic.*
- ▶ *As well as road traffic, you may have lots of human traffic to contend with on busy streets. Dodging in and out of crowds of people is not conducive to a good run – avoid busy high streets and schools at start and finish times. It's amazing how many people don't seem to notice you running towards or behind them, and fail to step out of the way or actually manage to collide with you, especially if your sudden advance makes them jump!*
- ▶ *Having a reasonably even surface doesn't mean there won't be kerbs and uneven pavements to watch out for. Be particularly careful towards the end of your run when you're getting tired and may not be picking your feet up high enough – concrete and tarmac are unforgiving surfaces to fall on.*

GOING OFF-ROAD

Cross-country running routes can provide the most enjoyable – and difficult – running routes. The surroundings are more stimulating and can provide more dissociation than a long, straight road, and you're guaranteed to have less traffic fumes and fewer people to contend with. Although there are drawbacks to off-road running, every regular runner will welcome an off-road route in their list of runs, even if this includes a park or field to run around.

Benefits of off-road running

The changing terrain on a cross-country route can provide variety that breaks up your run by giving you useful markers of where you are up to – for example, your first mile may be a canal towpath, followed by 20 minutes of pathways before you reach the bridge and come back through the fields...

- ✓ *Running on different terrains creates different training effects such as increased ankle stability as a result of running on uneven surfaces.*
- ✓ *Running on dirt tracks, paths and fields imparts much less impact on the foot and lower leg than running on concrete pavements and roads, making off-road running less likely to create injuries such as shin splints (see Chapter 7 for more information on common running injuries).*
- ✓ *You can plan an interesting running route by either using an OS map or just walking or running around your local countryside.*

Drawbacks of off-road running

- ▶ *Wet weather is not good news for off-road running. Apart from being messy, puddles and waterlogged muddy ground will slow you down and can be slippery.*
- ▶ *An off-road route is bound to be less 'trainer-friendly' as far as cleanliness and the appearance of your trainers goes. Be prepared to return from your run with your running shoes mud-splashed, coloured green with grass stains, and carrying blades of grass, grass seeds, sand, small pebbles, etc.*

- ▶ *These routes may be limited to daytime and summer months if there is only natural light available (however, changing your running routine throughout the year is a good idea to maintain interest and variety).*
- ▶ *Although there should be less human traffic than on a public road, you may be more likely to come across mountain bikers or dog walkers. Although the occasional dog might dislike runners, most dogs either want to run with you, or simply get in the way, resulting in you losing your pace or having to swiftly side step or jump over them! Many dog owners will hold their dog or make them sit still whilst you pass, but if you find you have chosen the local dog-walking route and the path is quite narrow, you may need to rethink your running route to enjoy a sustained pace.*
- ▶ *Depending upon your choice of off-road run, you may not be able to maintain a steady pace if you have farm gates to open and close or difficult underfoot terrain at times.*

RUNNING ON THE BEACH

There can be few images that motivate you to run more than those of running on a beach. Jogging alongside the surf with the sun shining and a gentle breeze in your face… running just doesn't get much better than that. However, the hardness of the sand will determine whether you enjoy a reduced-impact enjoyable run, or a high-intensity training session.

Benefits of beach running
- ✓ *Stimulating all your senses, beach running is guaranteed to increase your endorphin production and induce a powerful feel-good factor.*
- ✓ *Any run with a great view provides an element of dissociation – the view can take your mind off how far you have to run or flagging energy levels.*
- ✓ *Running on hard sand is enjoyable – the impact of your footfall is dissipated into the sand, creating less impact on the joints.*
- ✓ *Running on soft sand is very hard work and, whilst this may be a drawback for those new to running, this also presents a challenge if you're looking for a more demanding run or for a specific training effect.*

Drawbacks of beach running

▶ *Most sand is very difficult to run on, and you'll have to either alter the time you run to coincide with the tide, or become attuned to quickly finding a band of hard sand to run on. Dry and very wet sand are both very different running surfaces, making running, jogging, and even power-walking very difficult and extremely energy-sapping.*

▶ *If you run close to the water's edge you'll probably be running on a slope, not good for biomechanical efficiency or easy running. Either limit the section of beach running on a slope in your route, or make sure you run back along the same section of sand to counterbalance the effects of running on a camber.*

TREADMILL RUNNING

Most runners are outdoor runners, although there are some who choose to run on treadmills for some or all of their running. Although hardened runners will go out running in most types of weather, treadmills are certainly useful in bad weather and come with a range of additional benefits listed here that you may not have considered.

Benefits of treadmill running

✓ *If you prefer to stay dry when it's raining, run in air-conditioned environments when it's hot and in reasonable temperatures when it's freezing, treadmill running is the ideal solution. The treadmill – whether it's in your garage or at the local gym – provides the perfect alternative to braving the weather.*

✓ *Treadmill running provides a safer option for running in the dark if your usual country road route is unlit, or for lone female runners, particularly through the dark winter months.*

✓ *With space for your towel and water bottle, visual displays telling you your running speed, distance, heart rate and time elapsed, and a TV in front of you, treadmill running offers lots of added benefits!*

✓ *Treadmill running in a health club also provides many psychological tools that can help you stick with regular running, including a sociable environment, progress* information and several forms of dissociation (TVs, radio, music, other people to watch or talk to). If you have tried road running several times and found it difficult to stick with, maybe treadmill running will suit you better.

✓ If the treadmill is at the local gym or health club, you should also have the benefit of qualified fitness instructors and personal trainers. An expert in running can help you to set goals, provide information on running clubs and local events, and offer feedback on your running technique and footfall.

✓ Running with a mirror in front of you can be a great tool to correct poor body alignment and running technique. You may be able to do some DIY gait analysis if you know what you are looking for.

✓ The treadmill bed (the part you run on) is made to reduce the impact on your joints as you run, making treadmill running less likely to create injuries commonly caused by continued impact on hard running surfaces such as concrete.

✓ Some treadmills enable you to download your workout into a computer or kiosk facility at the gym, creating progress and information reports on your runs. However, with the right kit, you can also do this yourself using a home computer or the internet.

✓ There is no wind resistance on a treadmill, and running on the spot is slightly different from having to propel your body forwards along a road or path. Therefore, treadmill running can be a good starting point for beginner runners.

✓ As you can set the incline and speed of a treadmill, and there are no roads to cross, dogs to dodge or gates to open, you can get into and maintain a steady running pace on a treadmill.

✓ You can opt for pre-programmed interval training without having to use a heart rate monitor, foot pod or watch. You can also increase the intensity of each run at the touch of a button by advancing to the next level – the treadmill will automatically create a faster speed, reduced recovery sections and/or a higher incline. Information on creating your own interval training sessions during a run can be found in Chapter 7 'Running to suit you'.

Insight

Running indoors on a treadmill has a built-in benefit, or drawback, depending on how you look at it, as there is less air resistance indoors than outside. Whereas this can provide an easier run, it also reduces the training effects of your running, so if you want to match the speed of outdoor running, elevate the treadmill belt by one degree to compensate for less air resistance.

Drawbacks of treadmill running

▶ *Many, if not most, runners find having to run on the same spot looking at the same scenery boring, and find the treadmill no comparison to outdoor running.*

▶ *Unless you have a treadmill at home, you are restricted to gym opening times and are reliant upon a treadmill being available. Many gyms also cap the time you can spend on a treadmill, limiting your run time to 40 or maybe 20 minutes. You are also restricted to the speed of the treadmill, although most do go up to approximately 15 miles per hour.*

▶ *Some people look down at their feet when they run on a treadmill, which can throw the body out of alignment. Also, constantly adjusting the speed, incline and feedback displays on a treadmill can take your body out of alignment, which can be difficult, especially on machines that are not so quick to react to adjustments.*

OTHER RUNNING OPTIONS

Of course there are other places to run, such as running tracks, local parks or school fields, all with their own benefits and drawbacks. When choosing your running routes, consider what will be easy to get to. There's very little point having a great run that you have to drive 40 minutes to get to – the traffic and extra travelling time alone will create barriers in building a running habit. One of the best things about running as a form of exercise is that you can just step outside your front door and run from home, and when you get back you can relax in your own shower or bath rather than jostling for space in a health-club changing room.

Creating a menu of runs

There are benefits to having more than one route. Having three or four different running routes of differing distances, times and difficulty levels creates a more interesting and varied running programme, and helps to create different training effects. It also provides you with ready-made alternatives if you want to run for longer, or have less time. For example:

MON	TUES	WED	THURS	FRI	SAT	SUN
Quick treadmill run at lunch-time		Early morning beach run, 30 minutes		Easy after-work 4-mile run		Trail run, steady pace, 50 mins

As you become familiar with each route you'll get to know the easier stretches and more difficult bits, the parts that are more open to the elements, and the turning point when you know you're on the last leg. You can maximize motivation, variety and fitness benefits by incorporating different runs into your week:

- ✓ *Your running will be more interesting and enjoyable.*
- ✓ *You are less likely to become bored.*
- ✓ *A road run will help you to gain pace and fitness.*
- ✓ *Off-road trails can help to build ankle stability on uneven ground.*
- ✓ *Difficult terrain such as hill running or running on the beach will train your anaerobic energy systems – great for higher-intensity running whenever you need that extra spurt!*

Of course, you might have an off-road path that is flat and even, providing opportunity to maintain a good pace. Or perhaps an undulating road run that tests your anaerobic energy systems and leg power with every hill and provides downhill running training – which may be useful for some running events – after each exhausting peak.

If you are training for a specific event, your training should emulate the event run as closely as possible. In other words, practise what you will be doing in the event during your training runs – run the route itself if you can. See Chapter 9 'Training for an event' for more tips on running programmes for events and races.

CHOOSE A RUN WITH LANDMARKS

Try to find interesting routes when choosing your regular runs – there's nothing more difficult than running along a straight, long road when you're tired and lacking in motivation. Different scenery and/or different terrain underfoot makes a run much more interesting and enjoyable. Any run should have ready-made markers along the way that help you to know how far you have run or how far you have left to go. If you aren't wearing a gadget that is monitoring your pace, landmarks you reach such as a river, a telephone box or a road sign are welcome markers that will also enable you to time yourself.

For example, knowing that you usually run past a certain telephone box 20 minutes into a run gives you something to measure your performance against – a quick check of the time tells you whether you're running quicker or slower than usual. If you've got the energy, a slower time provides the opportunity for you to speed up and regain your usual pace, and a quicker time may motivate you to go for a personal best.

There are several motivational tools that you can put into practice on a run without having to purchase a single gadget:

▶ *Time how long it takes to get to certain spots, then check your time on each run.*
▶ *Have specific stretches where you 'open up' and sprint.*
▶ *Plan a section of fartlek (fast and slow sessions) on long, flat parts of the route.*
▶ *Have an easy section of your run when you check your posture and running form.*

58

- *Note quarter and halfway points on each run by either distance or time.*
- *Try and catch up with people walking (or running!) in the distance ahead of you.*
- *Note markers such as a road sign or tree to get to before you enjoy a little recovery jogging or walking.*

Recording your runs

Keeping a record of your runs isn't necessary for everyone, but is very useful for runners:

- *keen to see progression*
- *keen to achieve their running goals*
- *training for an event*
- *in need of motivation*
- *struggling to build a running habit.*

Recording information from your runs provides important information on your progress, which is motivating in itself and can help to build a regular running habit. It's great to see your runs logged on a calendar or in a running diary, especially when you can include a new personal best or a goal achieved. It also provides you with the information you need to set new running goals. Knowing how many runs you did last month, how far you ran or what your personal best time on your usual run is, all provide starting points upon which you can build your next goal.

WHAT SHOULD I RECORD?

Note down whatever is important to you, or things that help you to reach a goal or just keep going. You may want to record:

- *the number of runs you do each week*
- *how long it takes you to do each run*
- *your personal-best run times*

- *your average running pace or speed*
- *the distance run*
- *total minutes spent running*
- *calories used.*

If you are serious about your running and have entered into a race, or are simply a runner who likes gadgets, you might want to record a catalogue of information such as training heart rate, maximum heart rate, time it takes to return to resting pulse after your run (a measure of fitness), average pace, fastest pace, distance run and, of course, run time.

Training for a running event spans many different types of runner and running event, from a fun run to a half marathon. However, whatever the event, you will benefit from a progressive running programme that enables you to complete your chosen event successfully and enjoyably. Information from each run that you do will help you to monitor your speed and distance and adjust your running schedule accordingly.

LOGGING YOUR RUNS ONLINE

Many people choose to log information onto computers or internet sites, and there are a number of good running sites and programmes where you can log your runs, set run goals for yourself or take up running challenges with other runners. Information on some of these has been included in the 'Taking it further' section at the end of this book.

DIET AND RUNNING PERFORMANCE

In addition to the information you log about your run, you may find it useful to note how each run felt, and what you ate and drank each day. This enables an analysis of nutritional information that can be very useful for running events. Consuming the right foods and fluids before or during a run will certainly affect your running performance. More information on nutrition for running is included in Chapter 6 'Food and drink on the run'. You might want to log information such as:

▶ *food/fluid intake and how long before your run you consumed everything*
▶ *whether your food or drinks provided energy for your run or made it uncomfortable.*

Knowing certain information – which foods do/do not suit you; how long ahead you need to eat certain carbohydrate foods or meals in order for them to be fully digested before a run; how much fluid you need to take on board to be fully hydrated – will maximize your running success. Without logging this information for a period of time, you will be working in the dark as far as your nutritional running needs are concerned.

Insight

By keeping a note of foods and fluids consumed with your running log, you will be able to link certain foods, meals and fluid intakes with your best runs, your personal bests, your easiest and most difficult runs. Once you make these connections, you can fine-tune your diet to maximize your running training and event results.

Of course, a qualified sports nutritionist could be invaluable to you and your running. Details of how to find one are included in the Taking it further section at the end of this book.

So, you're kitted out, you've chosen your route and planned your runs into your week. It's definitely time to get running! As far as running gait and running form go, why not go for a run and see how you feel? It may give you some pointers as to whether you need to work on your body alignment and footfall, discussed in the next chapter.

THINGS TO REMEMBER

You might already be out there running, but if you need some final direction, here's your plan for success!

▶ *Decide which days and times you will be running and plan this into your diary. Re-read the guidelines in 'Fitting a run into your day' (page 41) to help you decide which time of day will suit you best, and, remember, if you're new to this, start out with a couple of runs a week.*

▶ *Decide on your running route(s) – walk or drive the route beforehand if you need to know the distance or time it might take. Again, if this is your first time running, aim for no more than a couple of miles. If you need inspiration, re-read the 'Where to run' section (page 48).*

▶ *Are you running alone or do you need to take someone else's availability into account?*

▶ *Plan your meals on running days to fit around your run, giving you ample energy beforehand, with plenty of time for digestion, and carbohydrate-rich meals after each run. See Chapter 6 'Food and drink on the run' for lots of meal ideas to feed your running habit.*

▶ *Plan your hydration strategy to ensure you are well hydrated before you begin each run, and take on board extra water after each run. Chapter 6 gives you hydration strategy tips and shows you how to calculate your fluid requirements.*

▶ *Don't forget to warm up before you start, or begin your 'run' with a good walking section. You'll find more guidance on warming up in the next chapter.*

▶ *If you haven't run before, or for a long time, don't try to run all the way – use recovery walking as much as you need to.*

▶ *Don't worry about cutting your run short if you feel you've been too ambitious – remember, less is more in the early days!*

▶ *Don't aim to run too fast, and stop if anything hurts or feels uncomfortable.*

▶ *After your first run or walk-run, rehydrate, stretch and note down your distance and time – you never know when you might start to get the bug for wanting a 'personal best'!*

4

Get set and go – from warm-up to cool-down

In this chapter you will learn:
- *how to warm up effectively*
- *how to do a body check to ensure good running form*
- *how to cool down and stretch.*

If you already knew the benefits of regular running, have your route planned and your running shoes ready, this may be your chosen starting point in this book. There are those that like to plan, and those that like to do, and if you are one of the latter, you'll be ready to get out running.

However, before you go, a quick look through this chapter will give you the following information:

- ▶ *tips on how to warm up effectively*
- ▶ *a guide to checking your body alignment before and during a run*
- ▶ *tips on footfall and running gait*
- ▶ *how to cool down at the end of your run*
- ▶ *stretches to do after your run.*

Warming up

Every run should begin with a warm-up that prepares the body for the exercise it is about to do. Warming up has several benefits:

✓ *It elevates your heart rate and breathing in readiness for running*
✓ *It increases the circulation of oxygen and nutrients for fuel around the body*
✓ *It prepares the muscles, tendons and ligaments for exercise, reducing the risk of a pulled muscle or torn ligament*
✓ *It elevates core body temperature.*

Evidence indicates that warming up allows you to exercise for longer, makes the exercise easier, enhances performance and reduces the risk of injury. It also provides useful time for mental focus on the run ahead. The easiest way to warm up is by starting off with a fast walk and then breaking into a slow jog after a few minutes. The jog should advance into your normal running pace after five to ten minutes, depending upon weather temperature and the type of run you are planning to do.

Insight

Remember, you need to spend longer warming up in cold weather (or if you are cold) than in warm conditions, and higher-intensity workouts such as speed sessions require a more thorough warm-up than that needed for a steady jog.

It may take up to a couple of miles before you are thoroughly warmed up – experienced runners may notice that running becomes easier and more fluid a couple of miles into the run. If you are returning to running and are currently running no more than two or three miles, you may be stopping just as you are warming up – listen to your body and, if you reach the end of your run but feel good, add on an extra lap – this may be the easiest lap of all!

STRETCHING

There has been much controversy over whether runners should or should not stretch during a warm-up. The majority of research signifies that the best time for stretching is after your run, for the following reasons:

- *At this time the muscles and tendons are warmed up and more receptive to effective stretching.*
- *Most research shows that stretching before a run does not reduce the risk of injury and can even increase it.*
- *Some research indicates that stretching before a run may even be detrimental to performance, particularly in sprinting.*

Some evidence shows that dynamic stretching can be beneficial as part of a warm-up – dynamic stretching is a way of stretching muscles with exaggerated, fluid movements that mimic the muscular movements of the chosen exercise, or at least take the relevant muscles into a stretched position whilst moving. For example, rather than hold a calf stretch you would step backwards into the calf stretch position, touch the heel down to the floor, but immediately bring the foot back to its starting point, and repeat several times with alternating legs. This repetitive movement also helps to increase body temperature and heart rate, and can be incorporated as part of a warm-up activity.

Other dynamic stretches for your warm-up:

- *As you walk, include a few high knee lifts.*
- *You can lift the knee and rotate the leg out to the side as you bring your foot back to the ground.*
- *Just before breaking into a slow jog, lengthen your walk stride and aim to keep the back heel on the ground until the last minute.*
- *During your slow jog, kick the heels up behind you a few times.*

If you have tight muscles, the best way to increase flexibility is through post-run stretching or with specific flexibility training (stretching sessions). However, if you have always stretched before running in the past and have not had any running injuries, you may want to stick with your tried-and-tested pre-run routine.

Checking posture

Checking your body alignment can help to improve your running form and technique. It's much easier to check your alignment just before you begin to run, and this provides two benefits:

✓ *It enables you to start your run with better posture, which will lead to better running form.*
✓ *It gives you a 'reference point' to come back to when you recheck your posture during your run, enabling you to re-relax your shoulders, re-engage abdominal muscles etc.*

Perform this posture check immediately before starting your run, and then check it throughout your warm-up jog and run. Note that any 'stretches' mentioned here are fluid movements, designed to release tension rather than stretch the muscle.

Here is a list of things to check to ensure a correct posture:

HEAD AND NECK

Your head should remain in alignment with your spine. Some people run with their head tipped back, and some seem to dip their head forward as if looking at the ground immediately in front of them whilst running. Aim to look a hundred metres ahead of you when running.

Before you run

To ease tension in the neck, relax your head to one side, feeling the stretch on the opposite side of the neck, then allow the head to roll forwards, releasing tension at the back of the neck, and finally take the head to the opposite side. Keep your shoulders relaxed throughout these movements.

During your run
Keep your head in line with your spine, and look at the road or path ahead of you.

UPPER BACK, SHOULDERS AND ARMS

Many of us have tight muscles around the shoulders and upper back that need relaxing before a run. These muscles are likely to be tense if you've spent all day driving, working at a desk or on a computer. As running predominantly uses muscles from the waist down, stretches for the upper body are often missed out, but a few large shoulder rolls can help to relieve tension in the neck, shoulder and upper back muscles.

Before you run
Take the shoulders up towards the ears, then roll the shoulders back and down as far as possible. Repeat this a few times in conjunction with some deep breathing.

During your run
Every few minutes, focus on where your shoulders are – try to relax the upper back muscles and drop the shoulders down, keeping these muscles as loose as possible. Your arms should ideally be bent at approximately 90 degrees, but make sure you are not clenching your fists or arms. Some runners use their arms to help power them through a run and others like to keep the arms relaxed. Any movement should be close to the side of the body; avoid sticking your elbows out or bringing your arms and hands in front of your body too much, as this twists the torso. Shaking the arms out every now and then will help to release any tension in this area.

CORE MUSCLES – LOWER BACK AND ABDOMINALS

These muscles are covered together, as the lumbar area of the back (the 'small' of your back) is often over-tight, especially if the opposing muscles – the abdominals – are not conditioned and have become weak. Unconditioned abdominal muscles allow much core stability work to fall to the lower back muscles, creating muscular imbalance and over-tight lumbar muscles.

Before you run
Perform the lower back 'cat' stretch shown later in this chapter to mobilize the lower back muscles and release tension in this area. During your posture check, make sure that your abdominal muscles are 'engaged' by tightening the abdominal muscles so that you feel like you have a mid-section like an iron bar – a strong core enables all other muscles to work more effectively and is the basis for good running form.

Insight
When we sit down we tend to 'switch off' our core stabilizing muscles, which results in a tight lower back and weak abdominals. If you spend many hours sitting at a desk, swap your chair for a Swiss ball as this will help to keep your abdominal muscles 'switched on' to help you maintain balance on the ball. This will greatly increase your core stability.

During your run
Try and imagine yourself 'running tall', lifting your upper body up out of the hips. This improves body alignment and positioning, and also enhances breathing. It's more difficult for your lungs and muscles to work effectively if you are 'slumped' down into your pelvic cavity.

Every few minutes, refocus on your abdominal muscles, making sure they are 'switched on' or 'engaged'. Don't save this just for when you are running – do this throughout the day. The more you do it, the more likely you are to keep your core muscles engaged and working effectively.

HIPS AND KNEES

Good hip and knee alignment is partly determined by joint placement (how the bones fit together at the joint), but is mostly affected by good muscle balance and posture. Look at your hips, knees and feet when you stand in front of a mirror – everything should be facing forwards. If this isn't the case, there are a few reasons why not:

▸ *It may be lazy posture – if so, you should be able to correct it without feeling too much tightness or discomfort*
▸ *It may be a muscular imbalance or over-tight muscles – if this is the case, you may not be able to straighten your limbs completely, or, if you can, it will feel very tight and may be uncomfortable*
▸ *You may have a joint placement that creates an inwardly rotated hip, or misaligned knee or foot.*

Poor alignment can be (and often is) a combination of these factors. A good stretching regime, rebalancing exercises and sports massages can all have a beneficial effect if done regularly. If you find that your hips, knees and ankles are not aligned, this will affect your running form but may not cause you any problems. It might be worth getting some advice from a physiotherapist or sports therapist to see if your running technique is affected, and find out whether you need to realign your joints.

Before your run
Make sure that you include stretches in your post-run stretch or flexibility training for the abductor (outer thigh) muscles and iliotibial band if these feel tight, as they are a common site of injury for runners, particularly women. You can find more information on these areas and stretches for them in Chapter 8 'Overcoming obstacles'.

During your run
Glance down at your knees and see if they are rotating inwards as your feet hit the ground. If they seem to be moving inwards rather than staying straight, you may need to obtain some professional advice on your running gait, especially if you begin to experience knee or hip problems.

Whether your legs and feet are mostly in front or behind your body will depend upon how fast you are running and what your running form or technique is – some experts say that having a full-body forward lean is the most natural way to run. Running in this way will place your legs more behind you and take some of the strain off the front thigh muscles. Whether you power through your runs by using your front thigh muscles or whether you do have a natural, effortless running style, it doesn't matter as long as you are comfortable with the way that you run and are not creating any injuries from poor running form.

Footfall and running gait

Your footfall or running gait is one of the most important things about your running form or technique – a poor footfall can twist knees and hips out of alignment and create problems anywhere from the foot to the hips (or even further up), and is the cause of many common running injuries.

A normal or 'neutral' foot strike will create even wear and tear on shoe soles and heels, and your footprint will show your toes and forefoot connected to the heel with a broad band on the outside of the footprint. If your footprint does not look like this, you may over-pronate (roll in) or under-pronate (or supinate – fail to roll in enough).

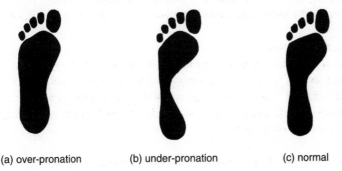

(a) over-pronation   (b) under-pronation   (c) normal

Figure 4.1 The three types of foot strike.

ANALYSING YOUR FOOT STRIKE

If the inside edges of your shoes wear out, this is an indication
that you over-pronate when you walk or run. Excessive pronation
causes the ankle and leg to twist and can lead to injuries such as
shin splints. If the outside edges of your shoes wear out, this is
an indication that you supinate or under-pronate when you walk
or run. This reduces the amount of shock absorbed through your
feet when you run, and excessive supination can lead to ankle
sprains, Achilles tendonitis, plantar fasciitis, and iliotibial band
syndrome.

HOW DOES THIS AFFECT MY RUNNING?

Your footfall affects two things:

1 *Your running gait.*
2 *The type of running shoe that will suit you best.*

If you don't know what your footfall is, an assistant at a
specialist running shop may be able to tell you by either looking
at your existing shoes or watching your walking or running
gait, and will be able to help you choose the best type of
running shoes.

Our feet should naturally roll inwards as they hit the ground, allowing the middle of the foot to absorb some of the impact. If you don't roll in far enough (under-pronate), or roll in too far (over-pronate), running shoes or orthotics can help to correct your footfall.

We all have our own way of running, although if you have not run since being at school you may feel as if you need to learn to run all over again! Your running form is important, as poor form can not only add minutes to your run time, but also cause running injuries, particularly those provoked through repetitive strain injuries. Incorrect footfall and poor body alignment are the most common things to affect good running form or technique, so spending time checking how you run is worthwhile.

Insight

Over-the-counter orthotics from specialist running shops can help – slip them into your running shoes and check for a more normal footprint to test them out. Alternatively, have your gait analysed by a podiatrist and get individual, custom-made orthotics. These cost more but are made to fit your feet.

Breathing tips

▶ *During jogging or running, expect to breathe through your mouth due to the exertion – this enables you to take more oxygen into the lungs.*
▶ *It's good to maintain a steady breathing rate, and you can even use your breathing to help set your running pace, or focus on it to get you through a tough stretch.*
▶ *Exhale fully as this will increase your next inhalation.*
▶ *Belly breathing (when the stomach rather than the chest pushes outwards with each breath) is said to help prevent or relieve side stitch whilst running.*

Cooling down

Cooling down enables the body to return to a pre-exercise state gradually, reducing the risk of light-headedness due to blood pooling in the veins. Continued but gentler movement facilitates the removal of waste products such as lactic acid from the muscles and allows your breathing, pulse rate and circulation to return to normal gradually.

To cool down, you can simply reduce your run to a slow jog and then walk for a few minutes, incorporating a few stretches along the way or stretching once you are home. If your run is timed right back to your front door, complete your run, log your time, and then walk around a little in the garden or up and down the road to cool down.

POST-RUN STRETCHING

Post-run stretching may form part of your cool-down if you don't have time during the week to do a stretching session at home, or take part in a flexibility session such as a stretch or yoga class. Cold muscles are not very receptive to stretching, so stretching immediately after your run is ideal if you feel you need to increase flexibility in any of your muscles.

Some research indicates that the least flexible runners have a more economical running style, but evidence also shows the following benefits from a regular flexibility session:

✓ *It helps to loosen over-tight muscles and ease tension.*
✓ *It can help to re-balance muscles and reduce injury.*
✓ *The overall effect can be improved posture and running form.*

✓ *You may even experience improved muscular power and an increase in sprinting speed.*

Stretches

Muscular tension and flexibility are specific to each individual muscle – for example, you may be very flexible in your quadriceps but have very tight calf muscles. Therefore, the main muscles to stretch are those that you need to stretch, although you could include all of the main muscles used in running. A stretch for each of these muscles is shown here.

CALF STRETCHES (GASTROCNEMIUS AND SOLEUS MUSCLES)

1 *Take a long step backwards so that your back heel is just touching the ground.*
2 *Make sure both feet are facing forwards.*
3 *Keep the front knee bent and the back leg straight.*
4 *Press down on the back heel, stepping back further if the heel easily touches the ground and no stretch is felt, and hold the stretch.*

5 *Change legs.*
6 *You can use a wall to provide stability and increased force through the stretch if you wish.*

Figure 4.2 Gastrocnemius and soleus.

Insight

To stretch the smaller, deeper soleus muscle in the calf, move the back foot a step in towards the supporting leg, bend both knees and adjust the body weight back slightly, sinking into the stretch. Hold and then change legs.

BACK THIGH MUSCLES (HAMSTRINGS)

(a)

(b)

Figure 4.3 Hamstrings stretch.

To avoid any strain on the knees, you can duplicate this stretch lying down on your back as in Figure 4.3(b), bending one knee towards your chest and holding it there with your hands. However, if it is easier, do this stretch from a standing position…

1 *Place one leg in front of the other and bend forwards from the hips.*
2 *Bend the back leg and keep the front leg straight.*
3 *Place your body weight on the bent leg and lower your torso until you feel a stretch at the back of your thigh in the straight leg.*
4 *Keep abdominal muscles tight to support the lower back as you lean forwards.*
5 *Hold the stretch, then change legs.*

Insight

To stretch the calf muscle (gastrocnemius) at the same time as the hamstrings, bring the toes up towards you on the straight leg whilst you are stretching.

FRONT THIGH MUSCLES (QUADRICEPS)

Figure 4.4 Quadriceps stretch.

1 *Stand against a wall or chair for balance and bend one knee, lifting your foot up behind you.*

2 *Hold the ankle if you can do so without twisting the body – if you can't reach the ankle simply keep the knee bent and push the front thigh backwards to increase the stretch.*

3 *Keep the supporting leg slightly bent so the knee is not 'locked out' as this places a strain on the supporting ligaments.*

4 *Keep abdominal muscles tight to support the lower back and help to avoid hyperextension of the lumbar spine (arching the back).*

5 *To increase the stretch and for good form, tilt the hips forwards.*

6 *Hold the stretch and then change legs.*

Insight

Avoid arching the lower back on the front thigh stretch by keeping the hips tilted forwards.

BOTTOM (GLUTEAL MUSCLES)

(a)

(b)

Figure 4.5 Gluteal muscles stretch.

1 *You can hold onto a chair or fence if you need to as you cross one leg across the other above the knee, and sink into a semi-seated position.*

2 *Do not bend the supporting leg more than 90 degrees.*

3 *Keep abdominal muscles tightened to support the lower back.*
4 *Hold the stretch and then change legs.*

To avoid any strain on the knees, you can duplicate this stretch lying down on your back as in Figure 4.5(b), crossing one leg over the other and bringing the bottom leg up off the floor towards your chest.

Insight

Increase the stretch on the smaller gluteal muscles by bringing the leg crossed over higher up the supporting thigh or sinking deeper into the squat position. Do not go lower than 90 degrees, and be careful if you have weak knees.

HIP FLEXOR MUSCLES (ILIOPSOAS)

Figure 4.6 Iliopsoas stretch.

1 *Take a long stride forwards keeping your front knee over your ankle.*
2 *You can keep the back leg off the floor or place the back knee lightly on the ground if you wish.*
3 *Tilt your hips slightly forwards until you feel a stretch down the front of the thigh stretched behind you.*
4 *Keep both hips facing forwards to avoid twisting the hips and back.*

INNER THIGH MUSCLES (ADDUCTORS)

Figure 4.7 Adductors stretch.

1 *Sit on the floor with your back straight and legs relaxed in front of you.*
2 *Place the soles of the feet together and let the knees drop to the side until you feel a stretch on the inner thigh muscles.*
3 *Hold this stretch, applying slight pressure to the thighs or knees with the hands if you want to increase the stretch.*

OUTER THIGH MUSCLES AND TENDON (ABDUCTORS AND ILIOTIBIAL BAND)

One of the outer thigh muscles, the tensor fascia latae, develops into a long tendon that travels down the outside of the leg.

Figure 4.8 Abductors and iliotibial band stretch.

This is known as the iliotibial band (IT band) as it attaches onto the ilium (hip bone) and the tibia (shin bone), and it often requires stretching in runners.

1 *Cross one leg across the front of the other.*
2 *Lean away from the hip that is crossed over until you feel a stretch in the outside of the hip and upper thigh.*
3 *Change legs.*

LOWER BACK

1 *Kneel down on your hands and knees, as shown in Figure 4.9.*
2 *Tighten the abdominal muscles to support the lower back.*
3 *Arch the back upwards as much as possible, bringing the head underneath and drawing the navel up and inwards.*
4 *Repeat several times.*

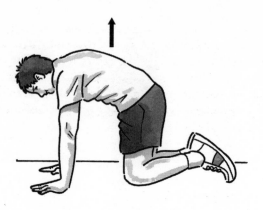

Figure 4.9 Lower back stretch.

FOCUS ON YOUR RUN WHILST YOU COOL DOWN

The cool-down is a good time to reflect upon your run:

▶ *How did you feel – were you energized or was it a struggle today?*
▶ *Can you pinpoint what might have made your run so much easier or more difficult?*
▶ *Did you try anything different and how did it work out?*
▶ *Have you got any sore or tight muscles that you need to stretch more?*
▶ *How was your run performance?*

or struggling with injuries or tight muscles, you need to find out why and make a change. If you don't address these things they will continue to make your runs hard work. Immediately after a run is the ideal time to consider how your run has gone and log vital information – if you don't do it now, you'll quickly forget how the run went and you may experience the same problems on your next run.

Rehydrate and refuel

You'll probably grab a glass of water as soon as you get in from a run, but after a hot shower or bath, the next thing on the post-run agenda is more rehydration and refuelling. It's essential to replenish both water and glycogen (stored carbohydrate) levels in preparation for your next run. See Chapter 6 'Food and drink on the run' for tips on post-run meals and hydration strategies.

THINGS TO REMEMBER

▶ *A quick body check before you start helps to remind you how to control your alignment whilst you are running.*

▶ *Warm up with a fast walk and large muscle movements to get the most out of your run.*

▶ *Start off slowly and ease into your run as if working through the gears on a car.*

▶ *Regularly check your footfall and body alignment for good running form.*

▶ *Stretch out muscles at the end of your run when they are warmed up and more flexible.*

5

Exercise psychology

In this chapter you will learn:
- *how to set and achieve running goals*
- *how to master the art of regular running*
- *how to use exercise dissociation to your advantage*
- *how to enjoy running and create a long-term running habit.*

Essential for all runners, this chapter explores exercise psychology, helping you to build and maintain a successful running habit. Up to 80 per cent of people do not have the 'self-management' skills to continue with regular exercise without some sort of support system – which explains why many of us stop and start running several times over the years.

Maintaining an exercise habit can be tough, and regular running is no exception. However, the good news is that there are lots of simple tools and tips that will help you to stick with your running for long enough until you get the 'running bug' and become addicted! You may already be using these techniques without realizing – take a look at this list and see if you recognize anything that has worked for you:

- ▶ *setting running goals*
- ▶ *measuring progress*
- ▶ *listening to music whilst running*

- *running with others*
- *entering a running event.*

These are all things that can help you to create a healthy running habit. Simply choose the things that work for you and create your own 'toolbox' of things to help you overcome obstacles.

Running is one of the most common activities started, yet regular runs often dwindle to a 'now and then' token effort within a matter of weeks or months. Although running is one of the easiest activities to begin – after all, you need only a pair of trainers and somewhere to run – it can also be one of the toughest types of exercise to do, and this is one of the main reasons why so many people give up before it gets easier. Moving your body weight through space at speed is no mean feat, and the difficulty level (perceived exertion) of any activity affects whether we enjoy it or not, and whether we stick with it.

Although warming up properly, recovery walking and good running form all make running less difficult, there are also a number of psychological techniques and tools you can use to help you create a regular running habit.

Dissociation

For some, being out of breath, feeling hot and sweaty, and exercising at a high intensity is not an enjoyable experience, and the only way to get through it is by doing something that takes your mind off the exercise. This is called dissociation – take a look at common methods of exercise dissociation:

- *listening to music whilst you run*
- *watching TV or listening to music in a gym*
- *chatting with a friend or running partner*
- *having a good running view e.g. a beach or mountain trail*

- *concentrating your mind on something else – revision, work problems, counting paces etc.*
- *tuning in to your body as you run.*

Dissociation takes your mind off the exercise you are doing and relieves boredom and/or exercise discomfort. For some people, this helps to get them through a run and contributes to building a regular running habit.

USEFUL DISSOCIATION

Some experts argue that our minds should be focused upon our running technique, and that dissociating ourselves from the run itself is counterproductive to good running form. If you are experiencing injuries from running, or trying to improve your running technique, this may certainly be the case. However, you can choose to focus upon the run itself as a form of dissociation by concentrating upon any of the following:

- *core strength – keep your abdominal muscles 'engaged'*
- *footfall – make sure the right part of the foot is hitting the ground – this will depend on whether you are a traditional 'heel-toe' runner or doing Pose or Chi running*
- *body positioning – check that your lower back isn't arched, your head hasn't begun to dip forwards, your knees aren't rotating inwards or that your upper back muscles haven't tensed up again*
- *breathing – you can control your breathing flow in time with your running strides*
- *interval training – running at different speeds for a specific distance or time gives you something to focus on during your run*
- *heart rate training – staying in different heart rate zones for different distances or times*
- *try out a new running technique such as Pose or Chi running (see the section devoted to these in Chapter 7 'Running to suit you').*

If you are trying to change long-term running habits or undo poor posture or running form, you need to constantly do a posture check throughout your run. Until your new posture and technique become habitual, it's easy to slip back into bad habits so you need to refocus on these every minute or so. More technical information on running form is included in Chapter 7 'Running to suit you'; it is mentioned here merely as a useful form of dissociation.

Running to music

Dissociation through listening to music has been labelled as both good and bad for exercise. On the plus side, it keeps us going; on the minus side it distracts our mind from focusing on what we are doing. However, one thing is certain – the many people who run with iPods and maintain a regular running habit must be doing something right! If you struggle to keep going, need extra motivation or something to take your mind off running, then music may be the answer for you.

Insight

If you are, or have been, a regular runner, you will probably have already experienced dissociation during a run – maybe when your mind has wandered onto something and before you know it your run is finished. You will have noticed that, whilst your mind was elsewhere, you didn't notice tired legs, lack of energy or the boring section of straight road that sometimes makes your run difficult. Dissociation works – try it!

Running with others

Up to 90 per cent of people prefer to exercise with others and, when we do, we are over 20 per cent more likely to stick with it. There are a number of reasons for this:

▶ *Dissociation – chatting to, or just being in the company of others helps to take our mind off the task in hand.*

- *Exercising with others provides an opportunity for social interaction, attaching more meaning and purpose to a run than just the exercise. Some runners regularly run with a running club as they enjoy seeing friends and running companions, the benefits of exercise taking a back seat to social interaction.*
- *Conscience and responsibility increase the likelihood of going for a run as you will not want to let a running partner down. This increases the amount of running that you do. If you struggle to motivate yourself to go out running, getting yourself a running partner or joining a running club may be the best thing you can do to create a good running habit.*
- *For some, the element of competition makes running more enjoyable and/or more effective, and, although you can be competitive with yourself with some clever goal setting, there's nothing like running with others to keep you on your toes!*

The best type of running partner for you will depend upon your running goals and your personality. For example, if you've entered into a half marathon with a friend, you have the same running goal and this can create a successful running partnership. Equally, if you want to begin running in order to lose weight and have a friend who also has a weight-loss goal, this too can work well. However, as well as considering the reason why you want to run, you should also consider your personality and running ability or level.

RUNNING WITH SOMEONE FASTER THAN YOU

If you enjoy being pushed, or are likely to take it too easy on yourself if you run alone, you may enjoy running with a faster runner, as this will increase your own pace and help to maximize your running and fitness potential. This could be someone who has done more running than you and is simply used to a faster pace and/or longer runs, or it may be that you begin running with a partner or friend who is also a novice runner but has a faster pace due to height or a longer stride.

'I'd love to run with my partner but he/she is much faster than me.'

If you and your partner are mismatched when it comes to running pace, there are a number of things you can do to provide both of you with a good run:

▶ The faster runner can insert sprints into the run, sprinting to a point in front or behind their running partner and then falling back into a slower pace when they return.

▶ If extra speed or distance is needed for one runner, they can simply 'open up' at the end of a run, or add on an extra lap or two. This works perfectly if you are both running back home, with the added bonus that access to the shower or bath is staggered between runners!

▶ If one runner wants to run a longer distance or include some higher-intensity running, they could also go out first and do a couple of laps at a faster pace, then pick up their running partner for a more relaxing second half. This can also even up the pace for the slower runner.

RUNNING WITH SOMEONE SLOWER THAN YOU

If you want to take your running at a steadier pace, and are likely to throw in the towel if pushed too much, partnering up with someone faster or fitter than you may be a disaster in the early months when you need motivation and positive running experiences.

Insight

It's better to run at a slower pace and still be enjoying it six months later than to begin at a pace that is too fast and give up after three weeks.

In contrast to partnering up with someone who runs at a slightly faster pace, you may enjoy the feel-good factor that comes from motivating someone else. Having a running partner with a slower pace can slow you down, but may also keep you going in the long run. Many people give up running because the perceived difficulty level is too high; it feels too hard and exercise discomfort is the reason for many running habits failing to form.

If this sounds familiar, choosing a running partner with a slower pace may be just what you need. It gives you a sense of responsibility to turn up for every arranged run; it provides dissociation from your own exercise discomfort whilst you motivate your running partner, and it gives you some healthy competition to remain as the pacesetter.

CREATING A RUNNING PARTNER OUT OF A NON-RUNNER

Unless your runs are a way of creating some personal space, it's great to have someone to run with and it can even prove to be a family occasion. If your partner runs considerably more slowly than you, or does not enjoy running that much, they may be able to match your pace on a bike. This could provide a fantastic training run for you, alongside a reasonably relaxing cycle ride for your partner. If you have young children, they could possibly join in on bicycles too whilst babies and toddlers could be pulled behind in a bicycle trailer. This is a win-win situation as:

✓ it is a great way to enjoy activity time as a family
✓ it enables both parents to exercise at the same time
✓ it creates healthy exercise habits for children
✓ it can provide a useful training session for you.

RUNNING CLUBS

Most towns have at least one running club, and such clubs will usually organize runs for beginners or novice runners as well as more demanding runs for regular runners. Don't be put off joining a running club by thinking that you cannot run fast enough or for long enough – every running club wants more members, and many of the runners probably joined as novices, so they will definitely cater for whatever level you are at. You should be able to find details of running clubs in the local paper, at the local gym or online. If your town or village doesn't have a running club... why don't you start one?

Virtual running clubs

There are several online running clubs and websites for runners that provide some of the benefits of a running club, though you still have to run on your own. Think about your reasons for wanting to join a club. If it is specifically to have others to run with, the virtual version will not appeal. However, for some friendly competition or a sociable outlet (even if it is mostly online), you might find that this type of running club suits you for a number of reasons:

- ✓ *You may be motivated to run more to keep up with the runs that other runners are posting on the website.*
- ✓ *You can enter team running challenges to complete a certain distance by a set date.*
- ✓ *You can socialize over the internet and via email – some runners may live locally enough for you to meet up occasionally.*
- ✓ *You can enter runs up and down the country with the running club – many runners travel to take part in running events and races.*

OTHER WAYS TO RUN WITH OTHERS

Most health clubs also have members' running clubs with weekly runs and, although you will be paying a monthly membership fee, you'll enjoy the added availability of treadmills in poor weather and access to fitness professionals who may be able to help you with your running goals, muscle imbalances, running form and entering into local events.

If all else fails and you want someone to run with but have failed to find a running partner or running club, why not employ the help of a personal trainer? Most personal trainers will plan your running routes, keep a check on your technique and run times, and of course provide motivation, dissociation and companionship during each run as well. You might need your personal trainer to run with you only once a week or once a fortnight to keep your motivation high enough to run several times in between on your own.

Alternatively, you could place an advert in the local paper to find a running partner, or choose to run at a local running hotspot where there are always several people running around the park or lake.

How to enjoy your running

Enjoying your runs will be the make or break of whether you stick with it or not. Quite simply, if we don't enjoy something, we don't do it! If you have to force yourself to get out there and run, creating a regular running habit is unlikely to happen – you are running for the wrong reasons. There are many different reasons for exercising, which can be split into extrinsic and intrinsic factors. Tick off any of the examples below to help you decide whether your motivations for running are, or have been, intrinsic or extrinsic:

INTRINSIC (YOU GAIN SATISFACTION FROM RUNNING ITSELF)
I enjoy the way running makes me feel. ☐
Regular running makes me feel healthier. ☐
Running energizes me. ☐

EXTRINSIC (YOU ARE RUNNING FOR A BENEFIT OTHER THAN RUNNING ITSELF)

I need to run to lose weight. ☐

I have to run to train for my event. ☐

I must start running to get in better shape. ☐

The difference between our motivations for running (or any exercise) is that extrinsic factors are less likely to help us stick with it in the long run. If you run because you feel you have to, ought to or should do, these are shaky grounds for a long-term running habit. If, however, you find your reasons for running are that you enjoy it, or you enjoy the way regular running makes you feel, these intrinsic factors are linked with a healthy, long-term habit.

Extrinsic factors may have motivated you to begin running in the first place, but if the end goal – for example, weight loss or improved body shape – is not forthcoming quickly enough, you will soon lose that motivation.

Insight

Having extrinsic factors or goals based upon changes in body shape are known as outcome goals or end goals, and, because it can take a while to achieve these goals, it may be difficult to maintain motivation in the meantime. You need to discover the joys of running for itself, because this will keep you running for long enough to achieve your other goals.

Enjoying running for running's sake is an intrinsic reason for donning your trainers – it's something that happens in the here and now, whenever you go out for a run, rather than a goal or outcome that is in the future. Quite simply, if you enjoy running, you don't need to have a specific reason to run or a specific goal. However, if you don't enjoy running for itself at the moment, you need to make some changes or you may soon be hanging up your running shoes.

Building a running habit

Many novice and returning runners will begin running but make the following mistakes:

▶ *overdo it to begin with and stop because of muscle soreness or injury*
▶ *try to run too quickly or too far, and find it too difficult to continue*
▶ *run too infrequently to create a running habit.*

You may have begun running several times in the past only to give up weeks or even months later because it didn't seem to be getting any easier or you didn't seem to be getting any better. With habitual running, it does get easier and it does become more enjoyable – you just have to employ the right tactics to get you through the initial period of adaptation.

Building a running habit may involve using all the tricks in the book – literally! You may need some form of dissociation from the actual running experience itself and you will need to set goals in order to programme regular runs into your week and motivate yourself to keep going.

Many novice runners 'turn a corner' in their running; this usually entails one or more of the following:

▶ *You suddenly find running easier.*
▶ *You can settle into a comfortable pace during a run.*
▶ *You have a regular weekly running plan.*
▶ *You may have specific running routes that you enjoy.*
▶ *You begin to have 'personal best' times for runs.*
▶ *You feel like a runner.*

OBSTACLES TO YOUR RUNNING HABIT

However, reaching this stage is not always easy, and many beginner, novice and returning runners drop out before they can enjoy the benefits of being a regular runner. Whilst we are building the running habit there are three main things that reduce the likeliness of sticking with running:

1 *You try too hard and dislike the exercise discomfort.*
2 *You don't plan runs into your day and fail to establish a running habit.*
3 *You don't do things that will make your run more enjoyable.*

Let's take a look at each of these barriers to see how to get past that all-important turning point after which running becomes much easier and more enjoyable, and you are more likely to want to run for the sake of running itself.

Trying too hard and disliking exercise discomfort

Running is one of the most demanding forms of exercise there is. There's no room to 'hide', no let- up, no 'breathers' – the whole run is on an intensity level that is tough to maintain... Well, your run is only like this if you make it like this! You wouldn't go into an advanced aerobics class if you hadn't done aerobics before; you wouldn't enroll in an advanced dance class if you had two left feet; and you wouldn't attempt to lift heavy weights if you were new to weight training. So, why try to run for miles flat out without stopping? Of course, we recognize and acknowledge running for what it is – running – and often fail to think that a slower jog or intervals of power-walking might be appropriate or helpful.

If you have never run before, have not run for a while, or if your fitness is poor, plan your introduction or re-introduction to running to accommodate this and you'll have a much more enjoyable initiation. If you think you are at risk of doing too much too soon, follow one of the running programmes for beginners or returning runners in Chapter 4 'Get set and go – from warm-up to cool-down'.

Poor planning and failing to establish a running habit

'Fail to plan, and plan to fail!' Lack of planning is the reason why many runners are not pounding the streets as often as they would like to be. It can be difficult to find time to run in a hectic lifestyle, but running is one of the easiest forms of exercise to fit into a busy day. The advantages of running over other types of exercise if you lack time are worth noting once more:

▶ *Running is an intense, effective form of exercise – you have to do less running than other types of exercise to enjoy the same training, fitness and weight-loss benefits.*
▶ *You can run anywhere, so whether you're on holiday, working away from home or staying with friends, all you need is your trainers!*
▶ *You can adapt your run to fit into your available time slot – enjoy longer, slower runs when you have more time, and fit in a faster, shorter run when you only have 20–30 minutes available.*

Ten top tips for creating a regular running habit

1 *Having a number of different routes providing differing run times and intensities will help you to plan runs into a busy day.*
2 *Be ready to take the opportunity for an unplanned run if a time slot appears in your day.*
3 *Be prepared to do a shorter run if you are late back from work or get up later in the morning – half an hour is better than nothing and will help to create the habit of getting out there and clocking up running time.*
4 *Consider your usual weekly routine and write planned runs in your diary – you have an appointment with your trainers!*
5 *Make arrangements with a running partner or join a running club. The added commitment will help you to stick with it as you're not just letting yourself down by missing a run.*
6 *Be prepared. Have spare kit at work, trainers packed in your travel bag, running shoes in the car, running kit laid out on the bed...*
7 *Don't allow your diet to let you down. Feeling lethargic because you haven't consumed enough water or carbohydrates will not get you off the starting block. Having enough energy is the first step towards feeling like running and having a great run. Plan your diet for the week to feed your*

(Contd)

running habit. See Chapter 6 'Food and drink on the run' for more information.

8 *Be decisive – just get out there and run! How many times have you stalled for time, wondering what the weather was going to do or trying to figure out if you have enough time to run? You're just looking for excuses, and the excuses usually win. If you find yourself dithering, just get your kit on and go.*

9 *Be your own psychologist! Negative thoughts thwart exercise plans on a daily basis – if you have some regular offenders, learn to recognize them and turn a negative into a positive. For example, how many times have you arrived home from work and thought, 'I know I should go out for a run, but I'm so tired. I'll run tomorrow morning instead.' More often than not, you don't run in the morning, so learn to reprogramme your thought processes when this excuse comes into your head by thinking, 'Yes I'm tired, but I know I'll feel energized if I run.'*

10 *Connect your runs to other things – it's your way of exercising the dog; it's your relaxation or personal time; it's the way you get to work and back every day (if you have shower facilities!).*

Not doing things that will help you to enjoy your run

Enjoyment is fundamental to success. If you are not enjoying your running, or have run in the past and not enjoyed it, you need to find out why. Once you have the answer to this, you can begin to find a solution.

If you have found running difficult in the past, you may be pushing yourself too hard or have a poor running form that is making running more difficult than it needs to be. You may find the run/walk options help in the early weeks until your fitness level improves.

Insight

The important thing to remember in the early days of running is that you need to build a running habit. 'You are what you do', which means you are only a runner if you run regularly. It doesn't matter how fast you run or what distance you run – you have just got to get out there. In the early days, it's all about just doing it!

HOW TO BUILD A SUCCESSFUL RUNNING HABIT

The diagram below shows how an exercise habit is created:

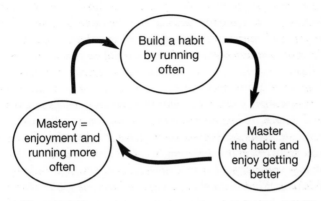

Figure 5.1 Building a running habit.

1 *First of all, you just have to run frequently, no matter how far or how fast. Get into the routine of going out for a run (or a run/walk) at least three times a week. You could use any of the dissociation or goal-setting tools to help you at this stage but, regardless of progression, this creates a habit, and from doing this repeatedly you will get better.*

2 *You will begin to find your running form and pace and start to feel more comfortable as you become fitter and run better; this is known as mastery. It's well known that when we master something, when we are good at something, we enjoy doing it so much more.*

Insight

Make a list of things that you are good at and a list of things you do regularly in your leisure time – you should find that your list overlaps, as the things you do regularly are the things you become good at (or master), and the things you excel at are the things you do on a regular basis.

'I'd love to run regularly but I get bored'

You may need exercise dissociation until you begin to enjoy running for itself. Have a look at these suggestions to see what might help.

- *Dissociation techniques such as running with others or listening to music will help make running more enjoyable.*
- *Think about where you run – maybe you need a new route or a number of routes to make your runs more interesting and keep motivation high. It's a good idea to have shorter and longer routes, and runs of different difficulty levels and times. In the same way that you change your food or your social habits to avoid getting bored, you should also adapt your running to keep it interesting.*
- *Setting yourself goals can also inject extra interest and motivation into each run – add on an extra lap, aim for a personal best or try a new running format such as interval training. See Chapter 3 'Planning for success' for ideas on different running routes and types of running for ideas.*

'I don't seem to be getting any better at it'

Very often the same run can feel more difficult than usual, yet, when you check your run time, you may find you have knocked minutes off your previous personal best. Of course, if you are not measuring these things, it will be very difficult to understand why it felt more challenging, or know how much you have improved. In order to know whether your running and/or fitness is improving, you have to have tangible things to measure your progress against. This in itself makes running more interesting and motivating, and can form the backbone of your running habit.

You could measure:

- *run times on each run that you regularly do (measuring speed)*
- *the distance run on each individual run or cumulative distance over a week or a month (increasing endurance or distance run)*
- *total time spent running (measuring endurance and running time)*
- *total number of runs per week or month.*

If running is a means to an end for you – i.e. you are running to achieve a goal such as weight loss – this could be the goal that you choose in order to measure your progress and success. For example:

- *measure weight loss or body fat lost if weight loss is your goal*
- *measure lung capacity or reduction in asthma medication if this was your reason for taking up running*
- *measure your progress towards a specific running distance (for an event) or running speed (for military, police or fire entry tests).*

Linking your running to something that is important to you can be very motivating, but to achieve a goal you have to set it in the first place. Goal setting is one of the most useful tools in building any type of exercise habit, especially running.

Setting SMART goals

Setting SMART goals can increase your chances of achieving your running goals by up to 20 per cent. Whether you have goals to help you build up a regular running habit or to help you train for an event, goal setting is central to success for many runners.

SMART stands for goals that are...

- *Specific*
- *Measurable*
- *Achievable*
- *Realistic*
- *Time-bound.*

CHOOSE YOUR SPECIFIC RUNNING GOAL

For example, this might be the total number of running minutes per week, the total distance run each week, or a personal best running time to be achieved by a certain date. Whatever your goal is, it should be very specific so that you know exactly what you are aiming to achieve. For example, 'Running more often' is not specific – there is no set goal to achieve, which will reduce motivation and focus, and you are much less likely to achieve your overall running goal.

MAKE SURE IT'S MEASURABLE

Your goal should be tangible and give you a definitive way of measuring your progress. During the early weeks of running it can sometimes feel like it isn't getting any easier, or that you aren't getting any fitter or faster. Having a measurable goal helps you to log your progress, and can be a very motivating tool, especially after a hard run.

Your choice of goal will define what you need to measure:

Goal	What to measure
Achieve a personal best (PB)	Time of a specific run route
Run a total number of minutes	Clock up the run time of each run
Run a specific distance	Note down the distance you run
Run a set distance in a set time	Note run time of a set distance

You will need a way of measuring these things, and some of the gadgets mentioned in Chapter 2 'Getting kitted out' will help to make goal setting easier and enjoyable, although you can also use a normal watch with a second hand or a stopwatch to enable you to time your runs accurately.

Insight

The problem with using a normal watch for timing your runs is that, as your mind drifts to other things during your run, it's easy to forget your exact start time. The last thing you want when you get back from a good run is deliberation over whether you started out at 5.15 or 5.20 p.m. Personal bests are often all about knocking seconds rather than minutes off your previous fastest time, so having an accurate timer is fundamental to success, especially as you get into your running.

You can also measure your total running time over the week or month, depending upon your goal – jot down the time of each run in a diary, a training log or on a calendar, or download your run information onto your computer or a running website. If you have a heart rate monitor or even a pedometer, there are a number of other things you could measure including calories used up, average heart rate or recovery rate.

Once you start to log your runs, you'll begin to see how motivating and effective setting goals and monitoring progress can be – it may be the key to success in maintaining a running habit or getting fit enough for a running event. If you are setting goals to help you train for a running event, you need to take account of the date of the event and what you need to achieve by that time. You will need to steadily adjust your running goals between the current date and event date. More information on training for an event can be found in Chapter 9 'Training for an event'.

MAKE SURE YOUR GOAL IS ACHIEVABLE AND REALISTIC

Although you will naturally want to see progress or results as quickly as possible, setting yourself an unrealistic goal is more likely to end in failure, which is demotivating and may be detrimental to building your running habit.

Insight

If you had decided to run four times a week but only managed to run three times, you may feel disappointed because you did not achieve your goal. However, if, considering what was achievable at your current level and with current work commitments etc., you had set a goal to run twice weekly and ran three times, you would feel motivated as you would have overachieved your target. The number of runs completed is the same in both examples, but the level of motivation and feeling of achievement are different, and may affect whether you continue with your running.

The idea is not to set a goal that is easy to achieve, but to decide upon an achievable, realistic running goal.

In order to decide what is achievable and realistic for you, remember to take into account:

▶ *what distance or how many runs/running minutes you are currently doing or what you have done in the past*
▶ *what your family, social and work commitments are over the next few weeks.*

We are often overly optimistic when setting goals, so it is worth planning how many runs you will complete each week, multiplying this by the number of weeks over which your goal extends, and then reducing the overall goal by one or two runs. Do not feel that this is limiting the number of runs that you can do – if you complete more runs than you originally planned for and overachieve your goal, this is very positive and motivating, and will fire your enthusiasm for running even further. Your next running goal can always be made more difficult.

Insight

Use total running minutes or miles for success. These goals are not dependant upon a set number of runs within any week – therefore you can play 'catch up' and still achieve your goal when you do have time for a longer run.

You could also decide to complete a specific number of runs, but make it over a month or six weeks – if you miss a run in the first week, it doesn't mean you have failed your goal at the outset, as you have a number of weeks in which you can catch up.

Goals like this concentrate your mind on the 'journey' rather than the destination, and are frequently used in sport and exercise.

MAKE IT TIME-BOUND TO MAKE IT WORK

The best time period for an effective goal has been determined to be between four and six weeks. Any less than four weeks can make it difficult to measure a sizeable achievement (especially with outcome goals such as fitness levels or weight loss), and any longer than six weeks may create delay in getting started (especially with cumulative goals such as total running time).

Insight

Once you have decided upon the date by which you will achieve your running goal, write it in your diary or training log, or mark it on the calendar. In fact, you should write out your goal in full – this is also thought to increase your chances of success, as is telling others about your goals. If you have an event that you are training for, this is a perfect date to aim for if it is within two months (obviously this may not be long enough if the event is longer than, say, 10 km, or if you have never run before).

Splitting larger goals into building blocks

Although you may have an end goal such as running a half marathon, this is too large to have as your initial goal – you cannot go from not running at all, or even running six miles twice weekly, to running over 13 miles in one go (well, you might, but you would know about it!). You aren't going to ignore your end goal; you are simply going to create achievable building blocks up to achieving that goal. Hence, the distance and speed you run at each week will reflect the improvements you need to make in order to be able to run a certain distance or speed on the day of your event.

Each goal you set will take into account your progress over the previous weeks, current fitness and how long until the date of your 'end goal'. The training programmes in Chapter 9 'Training for an event' will help you plan your running schedule, but here is an example of progressive, SMART goal setting:

Current running schedule/level Date: 1 May 2010	2 × 3-mile runs a week, taking 40 minutes each run
Goal – to complete a running event Date: 1 September 2010	10 km run in 50 minutes or less

1ST SMART GOAL
Gradually increase run distance on both runs to five miles by
18 June 2010.

2ND SMART GOAL
Do one extra run each week at same distance until 30 July 2010.

3RD SMART GOAL
Increase distance to 6.2 miles (10 km) on two runs weekly and
make one of these a timed run each week until race day. (The third
run can be a shorter recovery run.)

This means that by race day (1 September 2010) the runner will
have been running the distance necessary and timing some of the
10-km runs to ensure a run time of 50 minutes or less. By having
specific goals and monitoring progress towards each goal, you can
adapt your running schedule and goals accordingly to ensure that
you achieve your end goal.

OUTCOME GOALS V PROCESS GOALS

Although beneficial adaptations occur in your body from every
run that you do, actual changes can be difficult to measure or feel
early on. For example, losing body fat, improving lung efficiency,
improving recovery rate, or any of the physiological changes that
occur with regular running will not necessarily show a measurable
improvement within days or maybe even in the first few weeks.
Therefore, it is best to choose a process goal rather than focus
upon an outcome goal during the first few weeks of running.

Common outcome goals include:

- *losing weight*
- *improving recovery rate (the time it takes for your pulse to
  return to resting rate)*
- *achieving a specific training heart rate.*

Although these are all goals that can be measured and achieved,
because these physiological parameters are likely to change quite

slowly, it will be more motivating to measure the journey that helps you get to these goals, rather than measure the outcome goal, or destination itself.

For example, you may not notice much change in your training heart rate within six weeks, but you can achieve big differences in the total distance that you run, which is one of the things that will actually improve your training heart rate.

Insight

In choosing to measure part of the 'journey' rather than wait until the 'destination' goal, you will enjoy motivating results every week without having to wait to find out if you have achieved your outcome goal.

Additionally, if life gets in the way and affects your running plans, you can adjust your goal, managing your expectations and taking consideration of the bigger picture. All of these goal-setting tools increase your chances of successfully building a running habit, achieving a training effect or competing in a running event.

Examples of SMART goals

SPECIFIC	MEASURABLE	ACHIEVABLE & REALISTIC	TIME-BOUND
Complete 15 runs	Log your runs	This is a realistic average of 2.5 runs weekly	Runs to be completed by [date in 6 weeks' time]
Clock up 60 miles of running	Measure the distance run or know the distance of your route(s)	Accomplished by running 2 or 3 x 4-mile runs weekly	Distance to be completed by [date in 6 weeks' time]
Clock up 600 minutes of running	Log the time of each run	Running for 40 minutes, 2–3 times weekly	To be achieved by [date in 6 weeks' time]

Staying motivated with your running habit

Whether you have several weeks of running under your belt, are a regular runner lacking motivation, or are returning to running (again) after stopping and starting over the years, there are a number of motivation techniques and tools available to help you stick with running for years to come. Dissociation techniques and setting goals are not just for novice runners or for those training for events – there comes a time in every runner's life when extra motivation is needed to maintain the running habit.

This may come after a change in personal circumstances such as breaking up with a running partner, moving house and losing your old running routes, starting a more demanding job, having a baby, becoming injured or needing fresh motivation once an event has passed. Whatever the change was that affected your running regime, it's important to be aware of two things:

1 *Don't begin running at the same level as you left off.*
2 *Consider what stopped you running and work around it.*

DON'T BEGIN RUNNING AT THE SAME LEVEL AS YOU LEFT OFF

Training (fitness) adaptations disappear more quickly than they appear. Trying to run at the same pace or for the same distance as you used to is likely to demotivate you when you find it more difficult than anticipated. Consider how long it is since you last ran, and adjust your training schedule to suit – you will make quicker gains if you start out more slowly to begin with.

Having even short breaks of a couple of weeks between runs can mean you fail to improve, so don't be surprised at your lack of progress if you are not running regularly. Use the tips included throughout this book to help you build a regular running habit, and then continue using the techniques that suit you to maintain a long-term habit.

CONSIDER WHAT STOPPED YOU RUNNING AND WORK AROUND IT

If you can figure out why you stopped running, then you can find a way to work around it. Whether you had a recurring injury, got bored of the same old running route or changed your job and didn't have time for your long evening runs, there are tips and techniques throughout this book to help you get back into the running habit.

Insight

If you try to maintain your old running regime – the one that you stopped – it's unlikely you will be successful if the reason for stopping is still present (such as longer working hours). If you no longer have the time for a one-hour run, trying to fit it into your day will leave you frustrated at repeatedly failing to find the time to run. Fitting in more 20-minute runs throughout the week, however, creates a new running habit that can be sustained. Go with the flow! Sticking with any long-term exercise habit can be tough, and you aren't alone in finding it difficult! However, if you use the information in this chapter as your personal toolbox of tips to keep you going, you are more likely to be running for years to come.

THINGS TO REMEMBER

▶ *Get a running partner – it could reduce the risk of your running habit falling by the wayside by up to 22 per cent.*

▶ *Whatever you do, make sure you enjoy your running – if you don't enjoy it, you won't continue with it. Find running routes you love; run with people you like.*

▶ *Don't set yourself ridiculously tough goals – run because you want to, not because you ought to.*

▶ *Use music to motivate you!*

▶ *Set yourself SMART goals to stay motivated and keep a record of all those running achievements.*

▶ *Enter into a running event to give you something to aim for and set goals towards.*

▶ *Join a running club.*

So, choose the tip that does the trick for you… Set yourself running goals to keep going, listen to music or run with others to take your mind off the exercise, or sign up for a running event to stay motivated – simple suggestions, but all things that can help you to create and maintain a running habit.

6

Food and drink on the run

In this chapter you will learn:
- *how to time and choose your meals to suit your runs*
- *how to calculate your fluid requirements and make your own sports drinks*
- *how to manipulate your diet for peak performance.*

If you've already been out running before reading this chapter, you might have felt full of energy, or you may have felt as if you were 'running on empty', and that's the difference that eating the right foods, at the right time, can make. Your eating habits can make a difference to your running in more than one way:

▶ *Making sure you consume enough carbohydrate can make your runs so much easier and more enjoyable.*
▶ *Paying attention to your diet can make the difference between a tough slog and a personal best.*
▶ *Ensuring adequate fluid intake can transform your runs.*
▶ *The right nutrition will help you to win your running event.*

So read on to improve your general nutrition knowledge, and learn what you should be eating and drinking before and after each run. In addition, this chapter provides ideas for energy-rich snacks and meals, and lots of handy tools such as a glycaemic index reference table so you know how quickly carbohydrates will be digested and a formula to work out your personal fluid requirements, as well as a recipe for making your own sports drink.

Good sports nutrition can be the difference between giving up and sticking with it, or between losing and winning – if you're serious about running, you can't afford to skip this chapter!

The basics – carbohydrates, proteins and fats

Foods are broadly classified as being carbohydrate, protein or fat, although most foods are a mixture of these macronutrients. Have a look at the examples below so you can recognize foods that contain each nutrient:

Carbohydrate-rich foods	Protein-rich foods	Fat-rich foods
Bread	Meat	Vegetable oils
Cereals	Fish	Butter or margarine
Rice	Eggs	Fat in meat, eggs, fish
Pasta	Dairy foods	and dairy foods
Potatoes	Soya products	
Vegetables	Beans and pulses	

All three nutrients provide energy, but carbohydrate is the quickest and simplest fuel for us to use during exercise. Fat is a rich energy source, with nine calories in every gram of fat, compared with four calories in each gram of carbohydrate or protein. Although we can use protein for energy, it's mostly used when carbohydrate and fat are not readily available, and is generally not a preferred fuel.

We need carbohydrate, protein and fat (as well as fibre, water, vitamins and minerals) for good health and optimum exercise performance, so energy intake for those running regularly should be similar to the proportions suggested by the American College of Sports Medicine (2000) as shown below:

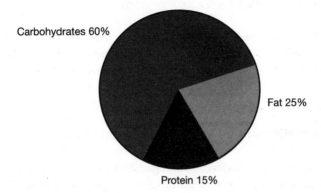

Figure 6.1 A healthy energy intake for a sportsperson.

CARBOHYDRATES

Carbohydrate foods are the main energy substrate for all exercise and activity. Daily requirements alter depending upon your body weight and how active you are – the more running you do, the more carbohydrates you should include in your diet.

Level of activity	Per cent of carbohydrate in food intake
Sedentary	50 per cent of total energy intake
Moderately active (several runs a week)	60 per cent of total energy intake
Endurance athlete (regularly running half marathons or more)	65–70 per cent of total energy intake

Follow these important guidelines to ensure that you are including enough carbohydrate in your diet:

▶ *Base each meal of the day on starchy carbohydrates – for example, porridge for breakfast, sandwiches or pasta for lunch, and rice for dinner.*

▶ *If you lack energy for your runs (before or during), eat more carbohydrates.*

PROTEIN

Nutrition for running has largely focused upon carbohydrate foods, with protein foods thought more important for those participating in strength, size or power sports. However, extra protein is required for endurance running for several purposes:

▶ *It enables recovery of muscles, tendons and connective tissue after running*
▶ *It maintains and promotes muscular strength for running*
▶ *After 60–90 minutes of running, amino acids are likely to be used for fuel and will need replacing*
▶ *It boosts immune function – particularly important for regular endurance runners*
▶ *It provides the protein and micronutrients required for oxygen transport.*

However, large amounts of protein consumed in one meal will simply be converted into fatty acids and utilized as energy or stored. Although the general guideline for protein requirements is 45 grams per day for women and 55.5 grams per day for men, you can calculate individual protein requirements based upon your body weight and sport, as shown here.

Activity level	Protein requirement
Normal	1.0 g per kg body weight
Endurance activity	1.2–1.4 g per kg body weight
Strength activity	1.2–1.7 g per kg body weight
Maximum	2.0 g per kg body weight

So a runner weighing 65 kilograms would need approximately 1.3 g × 65 kg = 84.5 grams of protein daily. This amount of protein in practical terms means eating the following foods during one day:

- *200 ml skimmed milk*   7 g
- *low-fat yoghurt*   7 g
- *small tin of tuna canned in brine*   24 g
- *chicken breast*   39 g
- *a handful of walnuts*   7 g

Including protein in each meal and in some snacks will enable you to meet your protein requirements. If you do not eat meat, fish, eggs or dairy produce, mixing vegetable protein foods such as grains and beans will provide you with complete protein.

Why do I need complete protein?

Proteins are made up of molecules called amino acids, and of the 20 or so that we regularly use, eight are essential in the diet as we cannot manufacture them in the body. It is ideal when all of these eight amino acids are eaten at approximately the same time, as the liver will have all the amino acids it needs for cell repair or other protein functions.

- *Foods containing all eight essential amino acids are called complete protein foods.*
- *Foods lacking in one or more of the essential amino acids are known as incomplete protein foods.*
- *Soya is the most complete vegetable protein source.*

Complete protein foods	Incomplete protein foods
Eggs	Beans and pulses
Meat	Vegetables
Fish	Cereals and grains
Dairy foods	

Combine grains such as wheat, corn or rice with beans or pulses for a meal containing complete protein – try these suggestions:

▶ *chilli with beans and rice*
▶ *beans on toast*
▶ *jacket potato with baked beans and sweetcorn.*

Even if you eat a little complete protein such as eggs and dairy produce, you will still benefit from combining beans and grains in other meals.

FAT

Fat is a concentrated energy source, and oily foods such as fish provide several essential nutrients. However, even though fat is a key fuel source during longer runs, it should provide no more than 25–30 per cent of your total calorie intake. Fat is used more during endurance events or runs of approximately one hour or more in duration – the longer the run, the more fat will be used for energy. However, fats can only be completely broken down with sufficient carbohydrate present. When glycogen (carbohydrate) stores are exhausted, fatigue is quickly felt, often known as 'hitting the wall', and exercise beyond this point is unlikely.

VITAMINS AND MINERALS

Adequate intake of the micronutrients (vitamins and minerals) is essential for good health and good running. For example, nutrients such as calcium, magnesium, sodium and potassium are essential for cardiovascular exercise, muscular contraction and fluid regulation, and several vitamins are required to convert food into energy.

A simple way to provide your body with the vitamins and minerals required is to base your diet on wholesome, unprocessed foods. Eating a junk food diet is like expecting your car to run on cheap petrol – here are some examples of the choices you could make for healthier nutrition and better-quality running choose:

- *jacket potatoes instead of chips*
- *a salmon steak instead of cod in batter*
- *fresh, lean meat over beefburgers*
- *wholemeal bread over white bread*
- *fruit or unsweetened oat/nut bars over sweets and chocolate.*

Nutrition for running

If you run regularly, you need to ensure that you are taking in enough energy. For example, it's a good idea to increase your carbohydrate intake up to 60 per cent of your calorie intake. Carbohydrates are found in foods such as bread, cereals, fruit and vegetables, potatoes, rice or pasta, and they are broken down during digestion into glucose, or stored as glycogen. We store enough carbohydrate as glycogen for approximately 90 minutes of exercise, and then we have to 'refuel' by eating.

FUELS USED DURING YOUR RUN

Carbohydrates are our most available fuel source, as glucose is constantly circulating in the bloodstream, making it immediately available and an obvious choice of fuel. It takes longer to access the energy in stored adipose tissue (fat), so fats contribute more energy later on in a run.

You can see from the following chart (Figure 6.2) that as carbohydrate (CHO) stores become low, more fat contributes to the 'fuel mix'. This chart simply provides a guideline of the proportions of fat and carbohydrate typically used over time, illustrating that more fat is used as glycogen stores reduce. The intensity (difficulty level) of a run affects the type and proportions of fuel used: the harder the run, the more quickly you use up carbohydrate.

Although a higher proportion of fat is used when we run at a lower intensity, more energy in total is used from both carbohydrate and fat during higher-intensity runs.

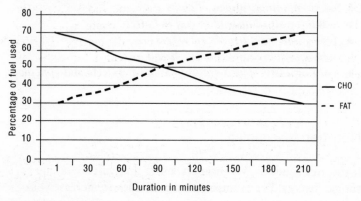

Figure 6.2 Proportions of carbohydrate and fat used during running.

Insight

A long, slow jog using approximately 600 calories may use 60 per cent of fat in the fuel mix (360 calories used from fat) but, because it is low-intensity exercise, fewer calories are used overall. A faster hour run using 1,100 calories may use less (40 per cent) fat in the fuel mix, but more calories are used overall. Forty per cent of 1,100 calories is 440 calories used from fat. So, although a higher proportion of fat is used for fuel in lower-intensity runs, more calories are used (overall and from fat) from a more difficult run. This does not mean that a long, steady jog is without its merits, but it may not be the most effective workout after all for 'fat burning'!

The glycaemic index

The type of carbohydrate you eat will affect your performance because different types of carbohydrate foods are digested and absorbed at different rates. This affects the amount of energy available and is used extensively in sports nutrition. Choosing the right carbohydrate foods to fuel your run is very important.

All foods containing glucose have a glycaemic index (GI) score. This relates to the amount of glucose a food contains, and how quickly blood glucose levels increase, providing energy. The foods with a high GI score are those that will provide a 'quick fix' of energy; those with a lower score take longer to digest and will provide energy for later in the day.

GI content of many common foods:

Food	Glycaemic index (GI)	Carbohydrate per portion (g)	Glycaemic load (GL)
Lucozade	95	40	38
White baguette	95	22	21
White rice	87	56	49
Rice cakes	85	6	5
Cornflakes	84	26	22
Gatorade	78	15	12
Watermelon	72	14	10
Mars bar	68	43	29
Digestive biscuits	59	10	6
Banana	55	23	12.5
Baked beans	48	31	15
Orange juice	46	14	6.5
Porridge	42	14	6
Spaghetti	41	49	20
Apple	38	12	4.5
Chick peas	33	24	5
Dried apricots	31	15	4

If foods have been digested in time to provide energy, or if your energy stores are adequate, you will have enough energy for your run. If energy stores are low, you may need to eat 'quick-release carbohydrates' for immediate energy.

GLYCAEMIC LOAD

The glycaemic load (GL) of a food relates to the effect that a
normal portion of the food or drink will have on blood sugar
levels, and takes into account not only what type of sugar or starch
a food contains but also how much glucose it contains (GI). It can
be calculated as follows:

$$\frac{\text{Glycaemic index (GI)} \times \text{the weight of available carbohydrate (g)}}{100}$$

For example, watermelon has a reasonably high GI as most of
the sugars are glucose. However, it doesn't have a high glycaemic
load as so much of it is water; a typical portion contains only
14 g of carbohydrate, in comparison to 40 g in a 250 ml bottle of
Lucozade. So if you are looking for something that will give you
a faster source of energy (and a reasonable amount of it), choose
a food or drink with a high GI and a high GL.

GI and GL – some useful pointers on what to look for

▶ A high GI indicates that energy will be released more quickly.
▶ A high GL indicates that the food contains lots of glucose
energy.
▶ A low GI indicates more starch than glucose and a slow
energy release.
▶ A low GL indicates not much glucose content to provide
energy.

High GI	70 to 100	**High GL**	20 or more
Medium GI	55 to 70	**Medium GL**	11 to 19
Low GI	Under 55	**Low GL**	10 or less

USING THE GI AND GL TO YOUR ADVANTAGE

You can use the absorption time of carbohydrate (GI) to:

▶ *provide energy just before your run*
▶ *provide 'top-up' energy during long runs*
▶ *provide slow-release energy for a run later in the day*
▶ *help you to adjust meals according to when your next run is.*

For example, an early-morning run would benefit from a carbohydrate-rich meal (high GL) the evening before, and, if there's time, a breakfast high in simple carbohydrates (high GI) to provide more immediate energy for the run.

If you are eating three hours or more before your run, you can choose a low-GI meal as it will be absorbed more slowly and provide a sustained energy release as you need it. Ideally, this will be a meal that is high in complex carbohydrates (high GL) to provide plenty of energy – including rice, pasta, beans or potatoes.

If you have only an hour or so before a run, go for a higher-GI meal as this will be absorbed more quickly and create available energy for your run.

Energy for your run

OPTIONS FOR AN EARLY-MORNING RUN
BEFORE BREAKFAST

▶ *Eat a carbohydrate-rich meal the night before, including foods such as potatoes, pasta or rice.*
▶ *Stay well hydrated through the evening as you won't get a chance to drink much the next morning.*

- Get up 30 minutes early to fit in time for a quick-release carbohydrate snack before your run, such as a glass of watermelon juice.
- Take an isotonic sport drink with you on long runs in case you run out of energy.
- Replenish energy levels after your run with cereals or toast.

OPTIONS FOR RUNNING DURING THE DAY BETWEEN MEALS

- Finish your last snack at least 90 minutes before you run.
- If you only have an hour before you run, keep what you eat simple and light, based on carbohydrate and avoiding high-fat foods or too much protein (as these take longer to digest). Try a bowl of cereal, a toasted bagel, or a little pasta with a tomato sauce.
- Ideally have your pre-run meal two to three hours before your run and top up fluid levels throughout the day.
- Replenish energy levels after your run with a meal containing both carbohydrate and protein.

OPTIONS FOR RUNNING IN THE EVENING

- Eat a slow-release (low-GI) carbohydrate-rich meal at lunchtime.
- A carbohydrate snack such as a cereal bar and banana mid-afternoon will help boost energy levels.
- Ensure good hydration throughout the day.
- If you are eating dinner before your run, consume a light meal with high-GI carbohydrates that can be digested, absorbed and used for energy during your run. You'll need to finish your pre-run meal at least 90 minutes before you run.
- Eat a carbohydrate-rich snack or supper such as rice pudding or a sandwich after your run and make sure you rehydrate. Snacks and meals should also contain some protein.

WHAT TO EAT IF ENERGY IS LOW BUT TIME IS SHORT BEFORE RUNNING

High-GI, easy-to-digest snacks are ideal if you have less than an hour before your run. These include:

- *fresh fruit smoothie (mixed berries and a banana)*
- *small portion of cornflakes, Rice Krispies, Weetabix (most processed breakfast cereals)*
- *fruit salad – banana, raisins, grapes, melon*
- *juiced watermelon.*

If you have one to two hours before a run, high-GI, easy-to-digest light meals will work well – for example:

- *tomatoes on toast*
- *toast with jam*
- *tomato or vegetable soup and a white bread roll*
- *potato salad with salad vegetables (skip the mayonnaise and salad dressing).*

MEALS FOR WHEN YOU HAVE MORE TIME BEFORE RUNNING

You should eat low-GI, higher-GL breakfasts or snacks that take longer to digest if you have one hour or more before your run. Try the following:

- *fresh fruit smoothie with added yoghurt*
- *fresh fruit salad (apple, orange segments, berries, kiwi, banana) with added yoghurt and topped with chopped nuts or seeds*
- *porridge with mixed nuts or seeds and a chopped banana*
- *toasted bagel with poached egg.*

If you have one to two hours before running have low-GI, higher-GL lunches and light meals that take slightly longer to digest – for example:

- *sardines on toast with a large mixed salad*
- *poached eggs and baked beans on wholemeal toast*

- *lentil soup and crusty rolls*
- *baked potato with tuna mayonnaise and salad.*

Finally, if you have up to three hours before a run you can try low-GI, higher-GL dinners or larger lunches:

- *spaghetti bolognaise (made with mince, turkey or soya)*
- *chilli con carne (made with soya, turkey or mince)*
- *lasagne (made with mince, turkey or soya)*
- *mixed-bean stew.*

Obviously, digestion times differ in each individual and also depend upon the amounts eaten and the way food is prepared and cooked, so try out different meals and pre-run timings and see what suits you.

Insight

Although every aspect of our diet affects exercise performance and recovery, carbohydrates and water are most likely to affect your running, as they both influence your energy levels.

- *If you haven't replenished your energy (glycogen) stores with carbohydrate foods, you won't have enough energy for a good run.*
- *If you haven't left enough time between eating your last meal and running, you're likely to have a poor run. Apart from just feeling uncomfortable, this may be due to lack of energy (as you haven't digested your food yet), and the dual demands of digestion and exercise placed upon your body at the same time.*
- *Dehydration can drastically reduce energy levels and limit exercise performance by up to 25 per cent.*

Adjusting your diet to suit your runs

The food that you eat will affect your runs, and the type of run you plan to do should determine your food choices. In addition to what you ate for your last meal and the timing of it, the fuel used during a run is dictated by several factors:

- ▶ *your fitness level*
- ▶ *how long you run for*
- ▶ *the difficulty level of the run.*

ADJUSTMENTS BASED ON YOUR FITNESS LEVEL

The more you weigh the more calories you use to run, so it is likely that you will lose some weight with regular running. As weight loss progresses, with a lower body weight, you will use fewer calories. If you have excess weight to lose, you shouldn't take in extra calories to accommodate the extra effort running will take in the first few weeks (or that will offset your weight loss!), but it's worth remembering that as you lose weight you will need less energy to do the same run.

If you are not used to regular running (or exercise) your body will take longer to replenish your glycogen stores from the carbohydrate foods in each meal. Therefore, you may need more time between runs to recover enough energy for your next run, particularly on longer runs.

ADJUSTMENTS FOR SHORTER OR LONGER RUNS

You can also adjust your diet to suit the length of time you spend running. For example, if your runs are up to 40 minutes long, you are using mostly carbohydrate in your 'fuel mix' and simply need to make sure you are taking in enough carbohydrate and energy for your needs.

Longer runs use more fat in the fuel mix and more energy (including carbohydrates) overall, so if you are including more than one long run (one hour or more) in your weekly running regime, you will need to eat a little more carbohydrate and also ensure you are getting sufficient protein and fat in your diet. Proteins are essential for muscular strength and cell repair, and help the body to recover from the demands of regular exercise.

ADJUSTMENTS ACCORDING TO HOW MUCH RUNNING YOU DO

One or two runs of up to 40 minutes should not noticeably affect your overall energy levels. However, several runs a week can deplete energy stores if you are not consuming enough carbohydrate. If you begin to feel tired towards the end of the week, or if the runs at the end of the week are never as fast or easy as the runs immediately after a couple of rest days, this may be an indication that you need more carbohydrate in your diet.

If you are a newcomer or returning to running, build up the number of runs you do each week gradually, as it will take your body longer to replace glycogen stores until the body has adapted. This is particularly important if you are completing longer runs of more than six miles.

Carbohydrate needs replenishing after every run, or energy stores become depleted. Full glycogen stores provide enough energy for approximately 90 minutes of exercise, so if you're feeling tired during your run, glycogen levels may have been low even before you began. The best time to replenish energy stores is within two hours after a run (see 'perfect post-run nutrition' later on in this chapter).

Insight

As a general rule, if you are feeling tired, or your runs become slower by the end of the week, you need to eat more carbohydrates. This is simply done – try the following ideas:

▸ *Add a banana to breakfast cereals*
▸ *Eat an extra spoonful of rice or pasta at lunch*
▸ *Add cereal bar snacks between meals.*

Just add one or two extra carbohydrate servings until you are eating an adequate amount to give you energy on your runs.

ADJUSTMENTS ACCORDING TO THE INTENSITY LEVEL OF YOUR RUN

The higher the intensity (how hard a run is), the more energy and carbohydrate you use up. If you're planning a high-intensity session, make sure pre-run meals are carbohydrate-rich.

Examples of higher-intensity runs are:

▶ *hill running*
▶ *running your usual route in a faster time*
▶ *sprints*
▶ *interval training*
▶ *adding extra distance to your normal run.*

Insight

There are two ways in which we replenish our energy for a run:

▶ *by eating carbohydrates to replenish our glycogen stores*
▶ *through resting between runs, allowing our muscles to store the energy we take in without using up too much.*

If you are planning a longer run or trying for a personal best, have an extra rest day beforehand – filling up on carbohydrates and allowing your muscles to rest and replenish energy stores will give you a better result on your tough run.

REFUELLING DURING A RUN

For runs of less than two hours, if you have allowed enough time between runs and eaten ample carbohydrate to replenish your glycogen stores, you should have enough energy. However, on longer or more challenging runs, or if glycogen stores were not fully replenished before your run, you may find you have to refuel during your run.

As attempting to eat and digest food whilst running is both difficult and unlikely to provide you with energy quickly enough, the way to take on board extra carbohydrate is in the form of energy drinks. These are discussed later on with hydration strategies, but, in short, the more glucose (or sugars) a drink contains, the longer it will take to be absorbed and affect your energy levels.

> **Insight**
>
> Only a limited amount of glucose can be utilized by the muscles when you are running and this may take up to 30 minutes to be digested, absorbed and fully available. Therefore, if you are running an endurance event, or think that you will have to top up your energy levels during any run, you should consume a sports drink *before* you need it.

Keeping a food diary and exercise log

You will soon make links between eating certain foods and how they affect your energy levels and running. However, if you don't write down what you ate and how the run went, you will easily forget. We all have slightly different digestion times and react differently to foods – one person may get a great energy boost from a plate of pasta an hour before a run, the next person may feel bloated. Learn what suits you and use it to your advantage!

Example of a food and exercise log

	Monday	Tuesday
Breakfast	No time	Porridge with banana
Lunch	Cheese sandwich and glass of milk	Lentil soup with crusty roll. Blueberry muffin. Afternoon snack – a cereal bar, glass of milk
Run	Ran before dinner. No energy. Took five minutes longer than usual.	Ran before dinner. Lots more energy. PB for four-mile route!

Optimum hydration

Although no single nutrient provides all the ingredients for success, optimum hydration is essential. We require between two and three litres of water daily to remain hydrated, and this is increased through exercise or in hot weather. About half of this fluid requirement comes from food.

If body weight is just 2 per cent lower through dehydration, this can decrease exercise performance by up to 20 per cent. This is often the explanation for a run feeling so much more difficult than usual, or simply taking longer. As a guideline, urine should be a pale straw colour, and water loss should be limited to 1 or 2 per cent of body weight. The first nutrient to be replaced after exercise should be water.

Insight

We've all had runs that, for no obvious reason, were more difficult than usual, yet the foods we've eaten, the running route, the time of day, have all been the same as normal. If this happens to you, think about how much you have had to drink over the previous 24 hours – dehydration may be the cause of these tougher-than-usual runs. Better still, keep a note of how much water you drink and aim to consume enough to keep your urine almost colourless... and then note how much easier your runs are!

HOW MUCH WATER DO I NEED?

The general recommendation is to drink one to two litres, or eight glasses of water a day. Ideally, diuretics such as caffeine-fuelled cola, coffee and tea should be limited as these also promote water loss through increased production of urine. To be more accurate and to calculate your individual requirements, you can base your water needs on your body weight as follows:

35 ml per kg body weight

So, if you weigh 60 kg you will need to consume approximately...

35 × 60 = 2,100 ml (2.1 litres) of water daily (from food and drink).

> **Insight**
>
> Any water loss through sweat can be measured by noting changes in body weight. Weigh yourself (naked if possible) before and after your run, ideally showering or wiping off any excess sweat before you weigh yourself post-run.

Drink about 1–1.5 litres of fluid for each kilogram (or 2.2 lbs) of weight lost, and keep on drinking until your urine returns to a pale yellow colour.

HOW TO REMAIN HYDRATED

Gulping down a pint of water before a run is not recommended. Some people cannot even consume a mouthful of water without feeling it sloshing about in their stomach whilst running, which can be a sign of dehydration through delayed stomach emptying. What's more, drinking in this way is unlikely to hydrate you in time for your run. Ideally, you need to meet your fluid requirements by consuming water and foods containing water throughout the day, well before your run.

Optimum hydration throughout the day is important as part of a healthy diet, and will ensure better performance rather than relying on drinking water just before or during a run. Drinking 500 ml of fluid in the two hours before your run will also help to ensure adequate hydration.

Top tips for staying hydrated

1 *Drink 1–2 litres of water/fluid throughout the day, every day, and drink an extra 1.5 litres of fluid for each kilogram (2.2 lbs) lost during your run.*
2 *If you struggle to drink ample amounts of fluid, fill up on foods with a high water content – e.g. fruits and vegetables, milk or soups.*

3 *Keep filled water bottles in the car and on your desk at work to provide ample opportunities to consume enough water throughout the day.*

4 *Remember to drink more in hot weather. But also be aware that we tend to feel less thirsty in cold weather; make sure you continue to stay well hydrated throughout winter months.*

5 *Always begin each run fully hydrated. Remember that thirst is not a good indicator of your body's fluid status; the sensation of thirst indicates the body is already dehydrated.*

Sports drinks

Most sports drinks aim to provide three nutrients – carbohydrates to replace energy, water to replace fluid, and electrolytes (minerals) to replace those lost in sweat. Glucose, sucrose or starch polymers such as maltodextrin are all used in sports drinks to provide energy. Sports drinks also often contain a range of minerals and vitamins, but most often include the electrolytes sodium and potassium. Both of these minerals are lost in sweat, and sodium also promotes the absorption of glucose and water in the digestive system.

Depending on the amount of glucose or other sugars in a drink, sports drinks can be used for hydration, for energy, or for both.

HYPOTONIC DRINKS – LESS THAN 4 g SUGARS PER 100 ml
- ▶ *These have a lower concentration of carbohydrates and are more diluted than isotonic or hypertonic sports drinks.*
- ▶ *Whereas water is ideal for shorter runs or when sweat losses are small, these drinks may encourage you to replace fluids through enhanced taste.*

ISOTONIC DRINKS – 4–8 g SUGARS PER 100 ml
- ▶ *These contain the same concentration of glucose to water as is found in blood, which enhances absorption.*
- ▶ *They usually also contain minerals such as sodium that can make them easier and quicker to be absorbed into the bloodstream.*

▶ *An isotonic drink is useful for longer runs when energy may need replenishing as well as fluid levels or during warmer weather when sweat loss is higher.*

HYPERTONIC DRINKS – MORE THAN 8 g SUGARS PER 100 ml
▶ *These contain more carbohydrate polymers and sugars, and have a slower absorption rate.*
▶ *They replenish carbohydrate stores, but are not ideal for immediate energy needs or rehydration as they take longer to be digested.*
▶ *Most fruit juices and canned drinks fall into this category.*

MAKING YOUR OWN SPORTS DRINK

Although sports drinks come in a variety of flavours with lots of added micronutrients, if you just want a drink that will replace fluid and carbohydrates, you can make your own 'sports drink' with water, fruit juice and an optional small pinch of salt (sodium chloride) in hot weather or after long runs. The sodium also enhances palatability of the sports drink and promotes fluid retention. Added sodium also helps to avoid hyponatraemia (low blood sodium), which can occur if sweat loss has been high and only plain water has been drunk, replacing fluid but not minerals.

Insight

Fruit juices with a high GI (high glucose concentration) are the best to use, such as grape juice or watermelon juice. Apple or orange juices have a lower GI, so they naturally contain less glucose and more fructose (fruit sugar) and may not raise energy levels as quickly. Experiment with different juices to see what suits your taste buds and energy needs.

The concentrations of hypotonic, isotonic and hypertonic drinks are shown in the table opposite. Just decide what your needs are – rehydration or energy replenishment – and add the right amount of juice to water for the desired concentration. These are approximate measures as different juices will contain different concentrations of glucose – read the label of the juice you plan to use to work out the concentration.

Type of drink	Concentration of sugars	Mix your own*
Hypotonic Less than 4 per cent sugar	2 per cent (2 g per 100 ml water)	Mix 200 ml of juice with 800 ml of water
Isotonic 4–8 per cent sugar	5 per cent (5 g per 100 ml water)	Mix 500 ml of juice with 500 ml of water
Hypertonic More than 8 per cent sugar	10 per cent (10 g per 100 ml water)	Drink juice as it is

*Based on a ready-to-drink fruit juice (not cordial) with 10 g sugars per 100 ml.

Deciding your energy and fluid requirements

Fluid or energy replenishment is not usually required during runs of up to an hour as long as hydration and energy stores are adequate. However, during longer runs, hotter weather or intense training sessions, you may need fluid or energy top-ups.

Drinking on the run needs some practice. You need a container that isn't too large, heavy or difficult to carry, and you need to practise taking small sips whilst running. You can buy water bottles with a hollow handgrip that are small and relatively easy to hold, or lightweight belts that will hold a small water container.

Many runners find carrying a bottle or trying to drink whilst running too clumsy, or find that drinking fluid whilst running doesn't agree with them. If you would rather not drink on the run, your pre-run hydration and nutrition must address your needs throughout the run. As you can see from the table below, you should only need to drink on the run...

- ▶ *during long runs*
- ▶ *during hot weather*
- ▶ *during higher-intensity runs.*

Run	Nutrition needs	Hydration needs
Up to 30 minutes Low intensity	Eat afterwards	Hydrate afterwards
30–60 minutes Low–medium intensity	Eat afterwards	Hydrate afterwards
30–60 minutes High intensity	A hypotonic sports drink would help rehydrate and replenish some energy	Small sips of water may be useful if the training allows – e.g. sprints on a field
1–2 hours Low–medium intensity	Using a hypotonic or isotonic sports drink will replenish both fluid and energy	Take a water bottle with you containing water, hypotonic or isotonic sports drink
1–2 hours High intensity	Using an isotonic sports drink will replenish both fluid and energy	Isotonic sports drinks will replace lost fluid and energy; alternate with water to rehydrate
Running in hot weather (if it's that hot, you're unlikely to be running for much more than 60 minutes unless in a race)	Electrolytes can be replaced with a hypotonic sports drink, and carbohydrate replenished from your post-run meal	For runs up to an hour, make sure you are well hydrated before you begin. Water or a hypotonic sports drink can be used to replace fluid

Run	Nutrition needs	Hydration needs
Running for 2 hours or more	Isotonic sports drinks will replenish fluid and energy during the run	Use isotonic drinks throughout your run

You need to refuel and rehydrate after any type of run – let's take a look at post-run nutrition.

Perfect post-run nutrition

There are two nutrients that must be replenished sooner rather than later after a run – water and carbohydrates. If your run was no longer than an hour it's likely that you haven't taken on board any water or fuel during the run, so fluid and carbohydrate stores need to be topped up. Even if you did consume both during your run, you will still have some replenishment to do, particularly after longer or higher-intensity runs that deplete energy and fluid reserves more completely and quickly.

Insight

To recover from the run you have just done, and to prepare properly for your next run, your post-run nutrition should be adjusted to match the distance and/or intensity of the run you have just done – for longer or harder runs, drink more fluid and eat more carbohydrate foods.

Any difference in body weight before and after a run is predominantly due to loss of fluid which needs replacing. You should ideally drink a pint of water for every pound of weight lost, or 1.5 litres for every kilogram lost, and keep consuming fluid throughout the rest of the day to rehydrate yourself fully.

THE IDEAL POST-RUN MEAL

Your post-run meal will ideally include some protein and be based upon a starchy carbohydrate food. For example:

▶ *fish or meat with potatoes and vegetables*
▶ *chicken, turkey, salmon or vegetable risotto*
▶ *tuna pasta bake*
▶ *chilli bean mix with rice.*

Remember, few foods contain only one single macronutrient, so you need to eat more than 100 g of a food containing carbohydrate to consume 100 g of carbohydrate, as not all of the food is carbohydrate – some will be fibre, protein or fat.

Ideally, you should continue to consume an additional 50 g of carbohydrates every two hours after your post-run meal. The following are ideas of what 50 g of carbohydrate looks like:

▶ *a filled bagel or pitta bread*
▶ *a piece of fruit and a Mars bar*
▶ *a mixed-bean salad.*

If you are unable to eat a full meal within two hours of your run, make sure you at least eat a carbohydrate-rich snack such as a sandwich, a bowl of cereal with milk and fruit, a milkshake or a high-energy sports bar, and then eat a normal meal later on. It also makes sense to adjust the amount you eat to suit how much energy you might have used up: a 20-minute run will not use as much energy as running for one hour, and a slow 45-minute jog will not use as many calories as completing a 10- kilometre run in that time. It can take as long as 48 hours to replenish glycogen stores fully, so continue to base meals and snacks on carbohydrates after your run.

Carbohydrate loading

'Carb loading' was originally developed to enable greater stores of glycogen to be stored for long-duration events (more than 90 minutes). It is used prior to endurance events such as half marathons or longer-distance runs where maximal glycogen storage and more energy are required. This is unlikely to be of much use for your usual runs if you are new to running, but may be useful if you get into endurance running. More information on carbohydrate loading is included in Chapter 9 'Training for an event'.

If you are interested in running events longer than a half marathon, why not take a look at *Be Your Best at Marathon Running* for some top tips and expert guidance. Details of this book are included in the Taking it further section on page 266.

SUPPLEMENTS AND ERGOGENIC AIDS

Whereas a nutritional supplement such as a multivitamin can help to provide optimum nutrition to support regular running, an ergogenic aid is assumed to enhance running performance significantly and several different ergogenic aids are used in competitive running. However, the average runner is more likely to use the following supplements to support and enhance their running:

▶ *sports drinks*
▶ *sports gels*
▶ *sports bars*
▶ *liquid meal supplements*
▶ *carbohydrate powders*
▶ *multivitamin/mineral supplements*
▶ *antioxidant supplements.*

A supplement should supplement a healthy diet rather than support an unhealthy diet. These are the first three things to evaluate when you are running regularly:

1 *Are you consuming enough carbohydrate for energy?*
2 *Are you consuming enough fluid to remain adequately hydrated?*
3 *Is your diet balanced and healthy?*

Make sure you can answer 'yes' to these three questions before you consider supplementing your diet. However, many of the supplements listed in the following table are extremely useful for supporting your diet, enhancing your runs as described.

Supplement	Benefit
Sports drinks	Sports drinks are useful for replenishing fluid and carbohydrate levels before, during and after running, or between meals.
Sports bars and gels	Bars and gels are useful for increasing carbohydrate intake between meals or after a run. Gels are particularly easy to carry on a run.
Liquid meal replacements	Meal replacements are useful when a healthy or adequate meal is unavailable (for example, when you are away from home). For those with a small appetite, a high-carbohydrate or high-calorie drink can provide extra energy between meals or after a run.
Multi-vitamins and multi-minerals	These are useful for ensuring that you take in adequate amounts of all the micronutrients. The better-quality food you eat, the lower your requirement for a supplement of this sort. However, regular running increases your need for these nutrients.
Antioxidants	Some research indicates that antioxidants can help to limit the free radical damage occurring during exercise, and may enhance recovery. Antioxidants also support immune function, which may be useful for endurance runners.

There are several ergogenic aids used in competitive running, including:

▶ *creatine*
▶ *amino acids such as glutamine*
▶ *caffeine.*

The ergogenic aid you are most likely to experiment with is caffeine. Caffeine is found in a wide range of everyday food and drinks such as coffee, tea, energy drinks and chocolate. As well as stimulating the nervous system, it enhances energy availability by increasing levels of glucose and fatty acids in the bloodstream. Consuming more than 5 mg per kilogram of body weight can create a glucose-sparing effect by increasing the amount of fat used for fuel, and research has shown benefits in both sprint events and endurance running.

The effect that caffeine has upon you will depend upon two things:

1 *How susceptible to the effects of caffeine you are.*
2 *How much caffeine you usually consume.*

How much caffeine do you need to have an ergogenic effect?

Amounts from 100 mg to 500 mg have been found to be effective, with no significant improvements from higher intakes. This equates to between one and five cups of coffee (more cups if you drink tea). However, if you don't normally drink coffee or tea, one cup might have a substantial effect upon your energy levels; if you regularly consume caffeinated drinks you'll probably need to drink more to achieve an effect. Caffeine doses as low as 1.5 mg per kilogram of body weight can produce energy spurts that will improve running performance.

From a health viewpoint you should not use caffeine to enhance your performance. Although caffeine can improve alertness and performance, it has no health benefits and has been found to increase blood pressure – not good if you do high-intensity running or racing. It is also a natural diuretic, so may contribute more to dehydration than to good hydration, and some individuals experience headaches, insomnia, restlessness or abdominal upsets through caffeine intake. However, if you drink coffee (or other caffeinated drinks) regularly anyway, you may be able to use your 'habit' to enhance your running.

USING CAFFEINE AS AN ERGOGENIC AID FOR YOUR RUNNING

▶ *Reduce your daily intake of caffeine – this way you are likely to feel the ergogenic benefits when you do drink it.*
▶ *Reducing coffee consumption will also decrease urinary loss of essential minerals such as potassium, magnesium and calcium – all necessary for optimum running performance.*
▶ *Drink an extra glass of water for each cup of tea or coffee you have to counter the diuretic effect on your fluid levels.*
▶ *Ensure that you are very well hydrated prior to using any caffeinated drinks for ergogenic benefits – remember that dehydration itself can sap energy levels, reducing your performance by up to 25 per cent.*
▶ *If you want to discover whether caffeine can have a beneficial effect on your energy levels, experiment by reducing your normal caffeine consumption and then drinking either a sports drink containing caffeine or one or two cups of coffee immediately before running.*
▶ *As with all adaptations to your diet, experiment with your training runs so that you know what works well before race day – you may find that drinking immediately before a run does not suit you.*
▶ *If drinking coffee, tea or caffeinated sports drinks does not have a detrimental effect on your run, you may benefit even more if you reduce your normal caffeine intake for a couple of weeks prior to race day and then consume your usual pre-run amount just before you race.*
▶ *If you are entering a running event, check if there are any rulings on acceptable caffeine levels in the urine – although consuming caffeine is legal, as an ergogenic aid it has previously been tested at certain race events and high levels found in urine may prevent you from running.*

Caffeine content of common beverages and foods:

Caffeine product	Caffeine content (mg)
Instant coffee	50–100 mg per cup
Filter coffee	60–120 mg per cup
Tea	30–60 mg per cup
Cola	50 mg per can
Chocolate	40 mg per 54 g bar

Source: *The Complete Guide to Sports Nutrition*, Anita Bean

THINGS TO REMEMBER

The better your daily nutrition, the more enhanced your running performance will be and the lower your need for ergogenic aids. Here are my top nutrition tips to keep you in good running form.

▶ *Make sure you stay constantly well hydrated – use the information under 'Optimum hydration' to calculate your daily fluid requirements and your additional needs after each run.*

▶ *Carbohydrates are a runner's best friend – include them in every meal and make sure you allow your glycogen stores to be replenished between runs.*

▶ *Make your meals match your runs – adapt your diet to suit the duration and intensity of your runs, particularly concentrating on fluid and carbohydrate intake.*

▶ *The quality of the food you eat will make a difference to the way that your body 'runs' – literally! Put in high-quality fuel for optimum performance.*

▶ *Use the glycaemic index (GI) of foods to your advantage – see the section on 'The glycaemic index' to find out which foods will give you fast energy when you need it, and what to eat when you've plenty of time to digest food.*

▶ *Practice makes perfect – always try out and evaluate dietary changes during training… not on race day!*

7

Running to suit you

In this chapter you will learn:
- *how to progress your running to the next level*
- *how to create a menu of runs*
- *about heart rate training*
- *different running techniques.*

Different running programmes and running methods suit different people; the important thing is to enjoy running throughout your life. There are many recommendations made by running experts, but one size does not fit all, and only by discovering what works for you will you build and maintain a healthy running habit. For example:

▶ *Some runners need to stretch over-tight muscles before they run; other runners have never stretched and have never sustained an injury.*
▶ *Some runners find they can increase their distance or pace by much more than the recommended maximum of 10 per cent per week with no problems whatsoever.*
▶ *Some runners have time for only one really long run a week, running far more than the recommended 30 per cent of total weekly distance in just one go, but this works for them.*
▶ *Many runners are happy running with a heel-toe footfall; some swear by the full body lean and landing on the mid-sole or forefoot.*

One thing is for certain, and that is that we are all different. We all need varying amounts of rest between runs or after races, we all respond to injuries differently, and we all progress at different rates. If you are an experienced runner, you will find that you can progress at a faster rate than that recommended, so you should adapt running programmes and advice accordingly.

This chapter presents many different options for running methods and running programmes, both for motivation and inspiration, and in an attempt to offer something for everyone. Just as some runners would not consider doing any other form of exercise, others welcome the variety that a cross-training programme can offer, and some runners cannot get by without incorporating flexibility or balance training into their regime. Hopefully, there is something for everyone in this chapter.

Progressing your running

As a regular runner, you have probably progressed from recovery walking and running one or two miles a week up to several regular runs, possibly up to ten kilometres in length or more. Some research suggests that, fitness-wise, once you can run continuously for 40 minutes or more, there is little need to increase your distance unless you have a specific event to train for. Running for 40 minutes can provide fitness and health benefits without overload or repetitive injuries.

However, any runner knows that, once you have run for 40 minutes, it's only a matter of time before you add on a couple more miles… but what comes next? Whether you're looking for motivation to keep running, inspiration for a more varied running programme, or ideas for your next running goal; whether you want to overhaul your running technique or have reached a 'sticking point', this chapter is packed with ideas to get you to the next level.

Creating a menu of runs

It suits some runners to do the same run several times weekly for several months or even years. This will maintain the level of fitness that this run requires, but will not provide variety or further training benefits. There are so many ways in which you can adapt your running regime, and this variety can be an important factor for several reasons:

- ✓ *It increases interest and motivation levels.*
- ✓ *It creates different training effects.*
- ✓ *It creates different runs for shorter or longer time slots.*
- ✓ *If you have hit a plateau and seem unable to increase your speed or distance, changing your running programme can be the catalyst your mind and body need to progress further.*

Adapting the types of running that you do is called cross-training, and the fitness and training benefits are well established in sport and exercise. Cross-training can even be useful during running injuries that prevent you from doing your normal runs. For example, you may be unable to complete long-distance runs due to an overuse injury, but may still be able to do hill runs or sprints. Cross-training can also mean doing different types of exercise in conjunction with running, but more about that later. For now, let's take a look at the different types of running you can do.

STEADY SESSIONS

Every runner should have one or more 'steady session' runs – these runs provide the backbone of your running programme, are likely to be on your doorstep, and, if you are a seasoned runner, may have been your first running routes to which you will have added additional circuits. Try to create a selection of three or four regular runs of different distances to provide variety in your weekly running programme. Your steady sessions may be a variety of road runs and off-road runs.

HILL RUNNING

Hill running increases the intensity of your run, which is useful when you want a tougher session, or if you have limited time and want to make the most of it. A hill run can be just as tough as a long-distance run of twice the distance, and regular hill running will make running on the flat feel effortless in comparison.

Of course, unless you are on a treadmill, what goes up must come down in any circular route, and downhill running also provides useful strengthening work for leg muscles. You could either choose a run with hills of different gradients throughout or find a hill to use specifically for hill work, running up as fast as you can and then jogging slowly back down again (unless you're training for fell running races where downhill speed is also important).

Your chosen hill for this type of work should take you from about half a minute to three minutes to run up, and the gradient should be tough enough to create a training effect, but not so steep that your running technique suffers. Hill running is a useful option to incorporate whenever you want to inject extra power into your running – the gradient makes the gluteal (bottom) and hamstring muscles at the back of your legs work harder as they power you up the hill. However, due to the muscles being lengthened whilst placed under stress on the downhill phase, be prepared for extra muscle soreness after a hill run!

Uphill running
Your pace will slow down as you go uphill, but try to:

▶ *maintain your rhythm*
▶ *shorten your stride*
▶ *stay at the same level of effort.*

Downhill running

You will be able to run faster downhill, but make sure you maintain control over your speed and running form:

▶ *Allow your stride to lengthen a little.*
▶ *If you are running off-road down a steep hill, try to run across the hill rather than straight down it.*
▶ *Keep an eye on where your feet will fall – running faster gives you less time to choose ideal foot placement and avoid obstacles.*

SPRINTS AND SPEED TRAINING

Speed training is also useful when you have less time available, as this is a higher-intensity session. Generally speaking, whenever the intensity of a run increases, the duration reduces, and vice versa. You can do sprints or speed training on your local field or park, at a running track, or maybe at the local leisure centre if the weather is bad.

Running at speed requires additional power from the leg muscles, and can enhance your overall running (through increased power) as well as hill running and sprinting. It increases fitness levels, trains the anaerobic energy systems that you use whenever you need to inject more speed or power into your run, and can also improve your running technique. If you are a regular runner, you may have noticed that your running technique is better when you run faster.

There are several ways to incorporate speed training into your running:

▶ *speed repetitions*
▶ *fartlek training*
▶ *interval training.*

Speed repetitions

A simple way to do a speed repetition session is to set up a distance between two points and time your sprint between these points. The sprint distance could be a 400-metre track or a 50-metre sprint between two posts, or you may base your speed training on a specific goal or event. A training partner or someone to act as 'coach' is useful during these sessions to act as motivator and timekeeper, and a running partner can also provide some competition.

It's always important to warm up before running, but it's essential before speed work as you are more likely to pull a muscle, ligament or tendon when running at speed. After warming up, simply time your sprint and do some recovery jogging in between sprints to keep your body warmed up and add to the overall training effect of the session. Try to better your sprint time with each effort – you will be surprised how many seconds you can knock off between your first and last sprint in a single session. You can plan your speed session to suit the time you have available. For example, a half-hour session might look like this:

1 *Warm up for ten minutes including jog around field/track/ sports hall.*
2 *Allow 20 seconds per sprint plus one minute recovery time = 80 seconds.*
3 *15 sprints plus recovery should take 20 minutes.*
4 *If you use a heart rate monitor, you should be working at approximately 85–95 per cent of your maximum heart rate during your sprints.*

Depending upon your running goals, you might want to include a speed session in your running programme once weekly, once fortnightly, or just every so often for a change. If you don't do speed work often, expect to experience some muscle soreness for a couple of days, particularly in the hip flexors, inner thighs, bottom muscles and calf muscles.

The bleep test – not for the faint-hearted!

This is a great way to test overall fitness, speed and endurance. You can purchase a bleep test CD or take part in a bleep test at your local gym or sports centre. You have to run over a predetermined distance (usually 15 or 20 metres) in an increasingly shorter time, reaching your marker before the 'bleep' sounds. The running speed usually begins at 8.5 km per hr (5.28 mph) and increases by 0.5 km per hr (0.3 mph) each minute. There are 23 levels, and you measure your fitness based upon which level you get to. You can convert your bleep test result into a VO2 max (fitness) score at www.topendsports.com. VO2 is a measure of the amount of oxygen you can take in and utilize in one minute; the fitter you are, the higher your VO2 score.

Some testers allow two 'fails' to reach the marker before you have to stop at that level. The bleep test is often used as part of the fitness test for entry into the fire service, police or military services; so, if you have taken up running to get fit for a new job such as any of these, planning a regular bleep test into your running programme is a good idea. Do check the exact protocol of the bleep test you are to be tested on, as different distances are used – for example, in the United States, 22 yards is sometimes used.

INCORPORATING SPEED WORK INTO YOUR NORMAL RUNS

Speed training doesn't have to be done in isolation from your normal runs, and running longer distances at an increased pace to normal has been found to increase fitness levels more than shorter, faster sprints. This type of running is also very effective for weight loss, as runners tend to use up more calories than they usually would by doing additional work during the faster intervals. Interval and fartlek training are very similar, although interval training is generally more structured.

Fartlek training

Fartlek is Swedish for 'speed play' and involves combining sprints with periods of easier recovery jogging. You can do this on any existing run by simply picking a point in front of you and sprinting to it (be realistic with the distance!), then recovery jog until you are ready to sprint again. You might choose to sprint on the more difficult or less interesting parts of a run to get past 'sticking points'. For example, sprint up hills that you usually find tough, or incorporate speed work into long stretches of road that seem to take for ever to reach the end of. Alternatively, you could use lampposts or houses to determine your sprint and recovery stop and start points.

Interval training

Interval running (also known as interval training) is very similar to fartlek training but tends to be a predetermined, timed programme. For example, after warming up you might sprint for one-minute intervals with three-minute recovery jogs in between.

You can use distance, time or heart rate to plan an interval training session:

- ▶ *Using distance, plan how far you aim to run at the faster and the recovery (slower) pace.*
- ▶ *Using time, plan how long you aim to run at the faster and the recovery pace.*
- ▶ *Using your heart rate (you will need a monitor), plan what heart rate you aim to get up to and how long you want to stay in that training zone before dropping down to a slower pace and reducing your heart rate. (More information on planning a heart rate training session is included later in this chapter.)*

All three types of interval listed above are easier to measure and monitor with the aid of a heart rate monitor, as you can pre-programme the distance, time or heart rate and respond to the bleeps on your watch (monitor) rather than try to guess distances or use a stopwatch. This type of running allows you to increase the intensity of your run without having to run faster throughout the entire run, which is tough!

As with all types of exercise, the training effects relate to the physiological demands placed upon the body; different benefits are gained from short, high-intensity sprints in comparison to more prolonged periods of running at a faster speed than your normal pace. Therefore, it's a good idea to try out both types of speed training, but probably not at the same time.

Sprint benefits	Benefits of prolonged bouts of faster running
Enhanced anaerobic energy systems	Enhanced aerobic and anaerobic energy systems
Improved speed and power	Enhanced endurance
Increased leg strength	Increased normal running pace
Increased running efficiency	Higher energy (calorie) usage
Improved running form	Improved running form

TREADMILL RUNNING

If you have access to a treadmill, you may want to use it for specific training sessions as you can plan the intensity and duration of the run to suit your needs as follows:

Goal	Treadmill benefits
Speed or interval session	You can choose an interval programme with set speeds and without having to time it yourself
Uphill training	You can set the treadmill belt at a specific gradient, or even adjust the gradient to suit, rather than rely upon the hills you come across in your run

Goal	Treadmill benefits
Heart rate training	You can monitor and view your heart rate easily, and adjust the speed and gradient to create specific training effects

Adapting your runs

To become fitter or improve your running, you must gradually increase your mileage, the number of weekly runs you do, or your speed. These are three running variables that come from the FIT principle, which stands for:

▶ *Frequency (number of runs weekly)*
▶ *Intensity (faster pace or more difficult runs)*
▶ *Time (how long you run for).*

However, when you have no spare time to do longer or additional runs this leaves intensity as the only variable left to change. This does not mean, however, that you have to increase your running pace.

There is an additional parameter sometimes added to the FIT principle, which is the Type of exercise done (FITT). A change in your running routine can increase the intensity and perceived exertion as much as an increase in speed and provide additional fitness and training benefits. For example, running the same distance and speed but choosing a different route can help to progress your running fitness.

As long as you are increasing, improving or changing one or more of these variables at any one time, you are progressing and achieving a running training effect, which means you are improving your running fitness.

Once you have reached a new level you can maintain that for a couple of weeks, but if you want to improve your fitness further, then you need to move forwards again by making a further change. If you are running for fitness benefits, six weeks should be the maximum length of time that you remain at the same level or on the same running programme. If, however, you run because you love running and have been quite happy running the same routes for months or years, then there may be no reason to change. Here's how the FITT principle works in practice.

CHANGING THE FREQUENCY OF YOUR RUNS

Week 1 – Complete two runs through the week.
Weeks 2 and 3 – Complete three runs through the week.
Weeks 4 and 5 – Complete four runs through the week.
Week 6 – Continue to complete four runs throughout the week.

Your goal might have been to build up to four runs a week, or to complete 20 runs over a six-week period. In achieving this goal, you have created a running habit as well as improving your fitness.

INCREASING THE INTENSITY OF YOUR RUNS

Week 1 – Run your four-mile route twice and time your runs to get a run time.
Week 2 – Run four miles in less than your average time (on each run if possible).
Week 3 – Add some interval training to one of your four-mile runs.
Week 4 – Do a timed four-mile run and try for a personal best.
Week 5 – Do two normal four-mile runs and one with interval training.
Week 6 – Aim for a personal best on your four-mile run and do an interval session on another run.

This six-week programme introduces interval training for variety and to improve speed, and also aims to improve the four-mile pace, setting a new personal best.

INCREASING THE DURATION OF YOUR RUNS

Week 1 – Run four miles three times through the week.
Week 2 – Run six miles once and four miles twice.
Weeks 3 and 4 – Run six miles twice and four miles once.
Weeks 5 and 6 – Run six miles three times through the week.

This running programme simply extends the length of the runs. Increasing your duration does not mean that you should run more slowly – stay at the same pace if you can, but simply add on an extra mile or two. It is a good routine to increase your run distance and note your run time, then gradually increase your pace and aim for a new personal best time for your longer-distance run.

Insight

A good goal during longer runs is to aim for the same pace (mile or kilometre per hour) that you run over shorter distances, which means you are maintaining your running pace and increasing your endurance. For example, if you run four miles in 40 minutes (ten minute per mile pace), aim to reach and maintain this pace over a longer distance: six miles at the same pace would take 60 minutes.

COMBINING FIT PRINCIPLES INTO A LONG-TERM RUNNING PROGRAMME

Mixing these different ways of progressing your running is a great way to promote variety, structure and goals in your running, whilst enjoying the fitness benefits that each change creates. Here is an example of how you can progress your running using different methods, with each type of progression building on the improved running regime you have newly created. Two weeks' maintenance is scheduled in between each progressive block to allow the body to adapt and avoid over-training.

Type of progression	Running adaptation	Time period
Frequency	To increase two runs a week to four a week Weeks 1 and 2 – Add one shorter run Weeks 3 and 4 – Make the new shorter run the same as your normal run Weeks 5 and 6 – Add an extra run	6 weeks
Maintenance	Maintain by running seven runs every fortnight	2 weeks
Intensity	To improve four-mile run time from 50 to 45 minutes Week 1 – Do a timed run Week 2 – Add interval training to one weekly run Week 3 – Make one run a hill run or sprints session Week 4 – Do one interval session and a timed run Week 5 – Do a hill run and an interval session Week 6 – Do one interval session and a timed run – aim for a PB!	6 weeks
Maintenance	Include one interval session weekly and try to keep timed runs faster than the original four-mile run time	2 weeks
Distance	To increase run distance from four miles to six miles Week 1 – Add an extra mile onto your normal run Week 2 – Maintain as in Week 1 (five miles, three times per week) Week 3 – Run five miles twice and six miles once Weeks 4 and 5 – Run five miles once and six miles twice Week 6 – Run six miles three times	6 weeks
Maintenance	Maintain runs at the new distance, seven runs a fortnight	2 weeks

This progressive programme takes 24 weeks – almost six months – to complete, yet there is a new running goal to achieve in most weeks. By the end of it, this runner would have:

✓ *increased run frequency from two to four times weekly*
✓ *increased run distance from eight to 18 miles a week*
✓ *increased speed by knocking five minutes off the normal run time.*

If you get to this stage and do not want to increase the frequency, time or distance of your runs, you can still progress by either increasing your speed (which means you can run further in the same time, hence increasing your distance anyway), or incorporate different routes or types of running into your training schedule. This brings us onto the fourth way to create a training effect – by adjusting the type of running that you do.

Insight

A simple way to change your run is to run your usual route the opposite way round. You'll be amazed at how different (and difficult!) this can feel, and it may be all you need to do to create the training effect or variety you were after.

Heart rate training

Heart rate training is a motivating, interactive way to run, and a great way to record and track your progress, although you will need to purchase a heart rate monitor. It's based upon measuring your heart rate and exercising in different heart rate 'training' zones at differing intensities. The more often you run at a specific intensity level, the fitter you will become at that intensity level.

To begin heart rate (HR) training, you need to calculate your predicted maximum heart rate so that you can run at different intensity levels such as 70 per cent of maximum heart rate (HR max). The simplest version of this calculation is:

$$220 - \text{Age in years} = \text{Maximum Heart Rate}$$

This should be enough for your needs, although this calculation may have the following inaccuracies:

▶ *It may overestimate HR max for those under 40*
▶ *It may underestimate HR max for those over 40.*

A more accurate calculation you can use is:

$$207 - (0.7 \times \text{Age in years}) = \text{Maximum Heart Rate}$$

So, if you are aged 40, your HR max calculation would be as follows:

1 *Calculate the section in brackets first: 0.7 × 40 = 28*
2 *Now deduct this figure from 207: 207 − 28 = 179 beats per minute – this is your predicted HR max*
3 *Now you can use this figure to calculate any HR training intensity as follows, although once you enter your age into your heart rate monitor it will probably do this automatically.*

Calculating a heart rate for a specific training zone

To calculate what your heart rate needs to be to work at 70 per cent of your maximum, simply multiply your HR max by the figure you want to work at and divide by 100 as follows:

$$\frac{179 \ (\text{HR max}) \times 70}{100} = 125 \text{ beats per minute}$$

WHAT ARE THE BENEFITS OF HEART RATE TRAINING?

If you are unsure whether your fitness is improving or not, want more specific fitness goals, or seem to have hit a sticking point, heart rate training could be the answer. There are many benefits to heart rate training:

✓ *You can measure any number of things such as your speed, distance, heart rate, recovery rate or calorie consumption – this enables you to set goals and monitor your progress.*
✓ *You can log and track your progress by downloading the information from each run onto a computer or a website.*
✓ *Measuring your heart rate enables you to see whether you are over-training, and you can check that your resting pulse is back to normal before your next run (sometimes, less is more!).*
✓ *Interval segments can be programmed based upon time, distance or heart rate.*
✓ *You can make interval training even more effective by basing your intervals on your heart rate and recovery rate.*

Here is just one example of a run based upon heart rate training:

Stage	Exercise requirement	Time
Before you begin	Warm-up	5–10 minutes
Stage 1	Start running at 70 per cent of your maximum heart rate	10 minutes
Stage 2	Increase your pace or incorporate a hill to elevate your heart rate to 85 per cent of your maximum heart rate	1 minute
Stage 3	Return to a jogging speed that reduces your heart rate to be at 70 per cent of your maximum heart rate	3 minutes
Stage 4	Repeat stages 2 and 3 for a number of times dependant upon how long your run is	
Stage 5	Finish with a section of recovery jogging and then cool down	

As your fitness improves your heart rate will decrease, enabling you to adapt your runs as follows:

▶ *Spend more time running at faster speeds as it will take longer to elevate your heart rate*
▶ *Adjust the ratio (1:3 – work:recovery) so that the recovery phase is shorter or the higher-intensity section is longer*
▶ *Add more of the work:recovery intervals for a longer run.*

Different running methods – Pose and Chi

If your joints are well aligned and you don't have a tight muscle in your body, or if running feels effortless to you and you have never experienced a running injury, then the chances are that you have good running form. But for the rest of us, good running technique may have to be learnt.

If any of the following apply, this section is for you:

▶ *You have just begun running and are finding it quite difficult.*
▶ *You think your running may benefit from a particular running method.*
▶ *You have encountered running injuries.*
▶ *You want to improve your running performance but have increased your pace, distance and duration as much as you can.*

There are two ways to adjust your running form:

1 *Focus on correct body alignment, good muscle balance and core stability, making posture and footfall checks throughout each run to ensure good form.*
2 *Adapt a specific running 'method' that may help you to improve your running technique.*

Traditionally, a typical running method has been that of a heel-toe footfall, aiming to:

▶ *run more frequently or for longer distances to build up running strength*

- *increase pace or speed*
- *gain more running power, speed, strength and/or endurance.*

Although not specifically a running 'method', this type of training is known as power-running, and is the way that most runners train and run, based upon the rule of overload:

> Run faster, longer or more frequently – create a training effect.

This is fine as long as:

- *over-training does not occur*
- *recovery is adequate*
- *quality of running is placed above quantity.*

There are alternative ways of achieving your running goals whilst potentially making running easier and improving your technique at the same time. However, relearning your running style is very difficult, and some coaches believe it can be impossible.

THE POSE METHOD OF RUNNING

The Pose method came about after Nicholas Romanov, a Russian coach, found that, as the running workload (distance or speed) of his athletes increased, so did the occurrence of injuries. He realized that most of the great runners had similarities in running technique and applied this to his running coaching.

The Pose method of running claims 'to make you more efficient, require less effort, lessen impact, and greatly reduce strains to muscles and connective tissues'. It is described as 'controlled falling'.

What is it?
- *You land on the mid-foot rather than the heel.*
- *Supporting joints are flexed at impact.*
- *The hamstring muscles contract to withdraw the foot from the ground.*
- *You rely on gravity to propel you forward.*

Heel-toe running

Figure 7.1 (a) Normal heel-toe running. (b) Pose running.

Features of Pose running

▶ *It has a shorter stride length.*
▶ *Vertical body movement is reduced.*
▶ *The runner 'falls' forwards allowing gravity to support the running motion.*
▶ *Legs remain behind or in line with the line of the body, placing emphasis upon removing the supporting foot from the ground and kicking the legs up behind you, rather than lifting and placing the thigh in front of you for your next step.*

How to Pose run

1 *Raise your ankle straight up under your hip, using the hamstrings.*
2 *Land on the balls of your feet.*
3 *Do not touch the ground with your heels.*
4 *Keep your ankle fixed at the same angle.*
5 *Keep your knees bent at all times, reducing normal standing height.*
6 *Keep your feet behind the vertical line going down through your knees.*
7 *Keep your stride length short.*
8 *Keep knees and thighs down, close together, and relaxed.*

9 *Always focus on pulling the foot from the ground, not on landing.*

10 *Allow gravity, not muscle action, to control the landing of the legs.*

11 *Keep shoulders, hips and ankles in vertical alignment.*

12 *Move your arms only for balance, not to produce force.*

Insight

The hardest part is often learning to flick the heel up towards the bottom as soon as the forefoot touches the ground, rather than pushing off with the toes. To master this movement, imagine you're running barefoot on broken glass or that you are running on a very hot surface.

Benefits of Pose running

✓ *Less vertical movement decreases the jolting effect of running, which could reduce the occurrence of side stitch and impact injuries.*

✓ *Eccentric muscle contractions are reduced, which should decrease post-run muscle soreness.*

✓ *Reduced impact on the knees may reduce the occurrence of knee injuries.*

✓ *A shorter stride length reduces potential overstretching of muscles and tendons, and may reduce injury.*

✓ *A forward lean enables some gravitational pull to increase pace with no additional muscular power required.*

Considerations...

▶ *If you have been heel-toe running for as long as you can remember, it will take considerable time and practice to change your running method to landing on the forefoot and not pushing off with the front foot.*

▶ *The Pose method requires considerable training in body alignment and correct positioning.*

▶ *This running technique is designed to reduce joint strain and is said to reduce impact by up to 30 per cent. However, it does require core strength, and better core strength in itself is likely to create better running form and reduce injuries.*

Insight

In Pose running it is essential to lean forwards from the ankles, keeping the rest of the body in a straight line. If you lean forwards from the hips or waist this puts additional strain on the lower back and creates poor alignment and bad running form. Practise the full body lean at home before trying it in your run, and ask a running partner or friend to assess your lean from the side. Here are a few practice routines:

▶ *Stand in front of a wall with feet hip distance apart and about a shoe length away from the wall.*
▶ *Engage your abdominal muscles to help you keep your body straight – your torso should feel like a rod of iron.*
▶ *Lean forwards from the ankles, keeping your heels firmly on the ground – your body should stay in a straight line, like a Nordic ski jumper.*
▶ *Practise this frequently, also with your feet together and with your weight first on one foot and then on the other, as you will be using a full body lean with your weight on only one foot whilst you are running.*

THE CHI METHOD OF RUNNING

Chi running was developed by the San Francisco coach and runner Danny Dryer, and is similar in many ways to Pose running. It employs a full body lean and uses gravity to make running easier. It enables you to enjoy running more and experience greater gains, although the emphasis is placed upon the quality of running form before building up quantity.

Chi running combines the mental focus and inner flow of t'ai chi with the power and energy of running, and can offer the following benefits:

✓ *It can reduce injury potential.*
✓ *It can reduce post-run recovery time.*
✓ *It can help to create an effective running training programme.*
✓ *It can make running easier.*

Features of Chi running

▶ *Chi running is based upon core muscle strength, allowing the leg muscles traditionally focused upon during running to relax.*

▶ *The runner must learn to relax all muscles (apart from the core muscles), rather than use arms and legs for increased power when running.*

▶ *It utilizes a full body lean that allows gravity to contribute to forward movement and make running seem easier.*

▶ *Emphasis is placed upon keeping the legs behind the body rather than lifting them in front of you.*

▶ *It encourages a flow and connection between mind and body: the mind is focusing upon and controlling the run; the body simply moves forwards under the gravitational pull created by the full body lean, and comes along for the ride! Obviously, in order to achieve this, you need to study and practice the Chi running technique.*

How to Chi run

1 *Perform a posture and alignment check before you begin to run.*
2 *Engage core abdominal muscles before and during your run.*
3 *Engage a full body lean from the ankles, keeping weight slightly forwards.*
4 *Have a mid-foot strike, landing on the part of your foot just behind the balls of your feet.*
5 *Keep knees pointing downwards and heels high behind you.*

Insight

As you lean forwards from the ankles, allow your legs to stay behind you to counterbalance your weight, opening up your stride behind you instead of in front. Keep your knees pointing downwards and your heels high behind you.

Benefits of Chi running

✓ *The reduced impact lowers the risk of injury.*
✓ *Use of gravity through full body lean makes running easier.*
✓ *It brings focus into your run, creating a useful type of dissociation that simultaneously improves running form.*
✓ *It focuses on good form and posture – quality over quantity.*
✓ *When the Chi running technique is mastered, the reduced effort involved in running will provide the ability to run further and faster.*

As with Pose running, Chi running requires considerable training in body alignment and correct positioning, and if you are a heel-toe runner it will take time and practice to change your running method to landing on the forefoot and not pushing off with the front foot.

If your running form is not good, there is little point trying to run faster or for longer, so good running form should remain the highest priority whatever running method you decide to try. Although some running methods, such as Chi running, are based upon improving running technique, it's important that you do master the technique correctly before you apply it to longer or faster runs, or you may increase rather than decrease your risk of injury.

Burnout and boredom

If you've reached a sticking point with your running, you should first determine the following.

Is it *physiological* (you aren't achieving new fitness goals and seem unable to run faster, longer or more often) or *psychological* (you aren't enjoying your runs as much – you need motivation or inspiration)? Working this out will help you to get past this sticking point and back to regular running...

GETTING PAST A PHYSIOLOGICAL STICKING POINT

If you are finding it difficult to progress in your running, or if your body is not responding to longer, faster or more difficult runs, it may be due to one of the following reasons:

▶ *You may need more rest to enable the body to recover and rebuild.*
▶ *You may be trying to progress too much or too quickly.*

If either of these is the case, revisit and adapt your running schedule using the running programmes and advice throughout this book.

▶ *You may have poor running form that is preventing you from progressing.*

If you suspect you may have poor running form, first try the alignment tips in Chapter 4 'Get set and go – from warm-up to cool-down', and get some professional advice from a sports physiotherapist or podiatrist.

GETTING PAST A PSYCHOLOGICAL STICKING POINT

If you are finding it tough to motivate yourself to run or simply not enjoying your runs as much as usual, it could be that:

▶ *You have been doing the same run(s) for too long*
▶ *You need specific goals to motivate you*
▶ *You would benefit from exercise dissociation.*

If you are lacking motivation or enjoyment, see Chapter 5 'Exercise psychology' for tips on goal setting and exercise dissociation. Whether the reason for your sticking point is physiological (in the body) or psychological (in the mind), passive or active rest may be the answer.

PASSIVE AND ACTIVE REST

If you have been doing more than four runs a week for a number of weeks, the chances are that you need a little more rest and recovery. You can do this in two ways, through more passive rest or active rest.

Passive rest will simply mean one or more of the following:

▶ *Reducing the number of runs that you do each week to allow longer recovery time between runs.*
▶ *Allowing longer recovery before and after your longest or toughest run.*
▶ *Considering taking a week or two off running.*

Active rest means resting from your normal running routine:

- *changing your run route, the distance and terrain to reduce intensity*
- *swapping to a different type of running that places more emphasis on different muscle groups – sprint training, fell running, track running...*
- *considering cross-training with other activities.*

A change is sometimes as good as a rest, and you may only need to change your running routine to get past a sticking point. However, if this doesn't work, you may need to incorporate different types of activity into your week – this can improve your running on a physiological and psychological basis.

Non-running cross-training options

If you love running, doing any other sort of exercise may not sound enticing. However, there are times when other types of exercise can offer a useful alternative to a run or actually enhance your running by improving cardiovascular fitness, strengthening muscles, improving core stability or increasing flexibility, and reducing the risk of injury.

CYCLING

Cycling is an effective cardiovascular endurance activity that provides a non-weight-bearing alternative to running. If you have an injury that is preventing you from running, you may find that you can still cycle, as no body weight is being placed upon the limbs and joints of the lower body. Take the advice of your sports injury therapist or physiotherapist and see how it feels. If you experience any pain or discomfort then you should discontinue, but otherwise, increased circulation to an injured area is often beneficial and will aid faster recovery.

SWIMMING AND ROWING

Swimming and rowing are also non-weight-bearing cardiovascular exercises, offering similar exercise benefits without putting weight onto the lower limbs. If cycling isn't a viable option, then one of these two activities can help to maintain cardiovascular fitness whilst taking the strain off the leg muscles (if that is where the injury is).

Remember that non-weight-bearing exercises utilize fewer calories as you do not have to support and carry your body weight, so to gain the same fitness or weight-loss benefits as running, you will have to do more cycling, swimming or rowing.

FITNESS CLASSES

In contrast to exercising through an injury, fitness classes can strengthen muscles, ligaments and joints and help to prevent common running injuries. For example, moving about in different directions in a fitness class helps to strengthen the ankle ligaments, reducing the risk of spraining an ankle on uneven ground whilst running. Also, specific classes concentrate on improving core strength or flexibility, and can be useful if either of these is your goal.

CIRCUIT TRAINING

Circuit training is often a higher-intensity session than fitness classes and usually incorporates some sprints or running around the outside of the circuits. A range of exercises such as press-ups, star jumps or burpees are done for an allotted time slot (approximately 30–60 seconds), interspersed with aerobic activity such as running. Although unlikely to be of use if you're nursing a running injury, a circuit class will enhance power, strength, endurance and cardiovascular fitness, and is a great alternative workout in bad weather.

WEIGHT TRAINING

Many runners avoid weight training because the more lean tissue you have, the heavier you are, and this obviously makes running more difficult. In addition to this, weight training promotes an increase in fast twitch muscle fibres (the type used for anaerobic activity), and unless you are a sprinter (which requires the power that anaerobic energy systems fuel) you need more slow twitch fibres for endurance running. However, apart from providing the type of muscle fibres that we need for sprinting and hill work, weight training offers a host of benefits for your running:

- ✓ It strengthens muscles, ligaments, tendons and joints, hence reducing the risk of injury.
- ✓ It can rebalance unbalanced muscle groups which would otherwise create poor running form and increase injury risk.
- ✓ If a full range of motion is used throughout each repetition, weight training can help to maintain and enhance flexibility.
- ✓ The increase in lean tissue increases metabolic rate, increasing energy consumption whatever you are doing (running, sleeping etc.), and this helps to reduce overall weight and body fat levels, contributing to easier running.

Just remember to keep the weights fairly light and the number of repetitions around 15–20 to avoid building too much muscle.

YOGA

Lack of flexibility is a common reason for poor running technique and running injuries, and, although many runners do a few quick stretches before or after a run, the muscles must be warmed up and each stretch held for at least 30 seconds and repeated frequently to increase flexibility. Yoga is one of the most effective ways to improve flexibility and has been found to enhance recovery rates after running. Yoga also incorporates the added benefits of enhanced breathing technique and mental focus – both useful tools for running.

PILATES

The importance of core stability for good running form cannot be overstated. There are many ways to tighten the abdominal (core) muscles such as abdominal crunches or Swiss ball classes, but

Pilates strengthens the core (mid-section) muscles in a functional way. Rather than shortening and lengthening the muscle (as crunches do), functional exercises work the muscle as it normally functions in the body. For example, our abdominal muscles don't shorten and lengthen constantly to keep our core strong; the muscles contract isometrically (staying the same length) to help stabilize our body, and Pilates exercises the core muscles in exactly this way. Without a strong core you risk problems such as an accentuated lumbar curve in your lower back, which tilts the hips out of place and affects running form.

What type of runner are you?

Are you an endurance runner or a sprinter? If you've been running for a while, you will probably know whether you are better at short, fast sprints or are more suited to endurance running. You may be equally good at both. The benefit of finding this out is that we tend to enjoy what we are best at, so, if you've been pounding the streets adding on miles and minutes to your runs and are finding the going getting tougher, it may be worth having a go at interval training or incorporating some sprint training into your programme. Alternatively, if you've been trying to increase your pace and are dreading your runs, easing back on the speed and adding a few extra miles could be your utopia!

WHY DO DIFFERENT TYPES OF RUNNING SUIT DIFFERENT PEOPLE?

Some muscle fibres are fast twitch muscle fibres and are used during higher-intensity exercise such as sprints or hill running; other muscle fibres are slow twitch and these are used in endurance exercise. Although there are a number of muscle fibres that adapt to the type of running we do (known as a training effect), if you still have more slow twitch fibres, you will always be better at endurance running, and if you are blessed with more fast twitch fibres, you should be sprinting!

Adapting your runs if you're better at endurance running...
- ▶ *Increase duration or distance rather than speed.*
- ▶ *Work in lower heart rate zones during interval training.*
- ▶ *Consider entering duration events such as half marathons.*

Adapting your runs if you excel at high intensity exercise...
- ▶ *Include interval or fartlek training in longer runs.*
- ▶ *Add sprint sessions to your running schedule.*
- ▶ *Try higher intensity options such as hill runs.*
- ▶ *Do your usual runs but aim for faster times.*

Whatever type of running you enjoy the most, whatever running method suits you best, the most important thing is to enjoy many years of running. For some of us this requires a changing menu of different runs, the latest gadgets, or technical running; for others it simply requires good running form, freedom from injury and time to run. The important thing is to discover what type of runner you are.

THINGS TO REMEMBER

Here's a reminder of just some of the options you have to ensure running enjoyment and progression for many years.

▶ *Create a menu of runs around you – uphill runs, cross-country jogs, sprints on the local field, laps around the block...*

▶ *Try a bleep test!*

▶ *Interval training has been proven to be an effective tool for superior fitness training and weight loss, and it also creates interesting and demanding running sessions – revisit this section if you've not already created your own interval training runs. Remember, you can use speed, distance, time, heart rate, calorie usage...*

▶ *Don't forget to use the FITT principle – Frequency, Intensity, Time and Type – to help you set running goals and progress your running fitness.*

▶ *Add a heart rate monitor to your next Christmas list!*

▶ *If you're struggling with constant running injuries or think your running gait or posture are not what they should be, try Pose or Chi running.*

▶ *Never underestimate the benefits of cross-training – sometimes, not running is what you need to get you back into running.*

8

Overcoming obstacles

In this chapter you will learn:
- *how to avoid running injuries*
- *what to do if you have a running injury*
- *how to adapt running to suit your health.*

Throughout any runner's life, things will crop up that affect your running such as side stitch, injuries, pregnancy, hay fever during the summer or health conditions. The good news is that you can usually adjust your running or running schedule to accommodate most changes in your health.

Some say that runners are either recovering from an injury, running through an injury, or just about to have an injury. However, it is not the running that causes the injury – it's your running programme or the way that you run! This chapter discusses tips and techniques to reduce your risk of injury, get you back on track as soon as possible, and provide you with a healthy, long-term running habit.

Insight
Three things you can do to reduce your risk of injury:

1 *Always warm up with walking and slow jogging.*
2 *Begin your run time after warming up to avoid starting runs too quickly.*
3 *Don't run too much – over-training increases your risk of injury.*

Common running ailments

If you are unfamiliar with the workings of your body, getting side stitch, a muscle cramp or post-running soreness can be worrying and off-putting. By understanding why these things sometimes happen, what they are, and how to avoid them or cope with them when they do occur, you can deal with them more effectively. To begin with, let's take a look at some of the problems that often occur during a run, such as muscle cramp and side stitch.

MUSCLE CRAMP

Exercise-induced muscle cramp occurs either during or just after running, often in the gastrocnemius (large calf muscle), quadriceps (front thigh) or hamstrings (back of the thigh). It is due to muscles contracting involuntarily without relaxing, and may last for a few seconds or for several minutes, either easing off or occasionally recurring several times.

What causes muscle cramps?
The exact cause is not known but several factors seem to contribute to exercise-induced cramp:

▶ *running at a faster pace or for a longer distance than usual (sprints and marathons)*
▶ *not stretching before or after running in some runners*
▶ *mineral imbalances due to a poor diet or after heavy sweating*
▶ *dehydration*
▶ *low blood sugar.*

How can I prevent muscle cramps?
▶ *If you have tight muscles, include flexibility training in your weekly routine, and stretch the muscles that tend to cramp after each run.*
▶ *Make sure you're not dehydrated as this influences levels of fluid and mineral salts in the body and affects muscular contraction.*

- Eat a balanced diet – muscle cramps may be due to deficiencies of calcium, magnesium, potassium or sodium as these minerals all play a part in muscular contraction.
- Consume plenty of slow-release carbohydrates throughout the day to keep blood sugar levels stable and to provide energy for muscular contraction.
- If you are planning a longer or faster run than usual, pay even more attention to these cramp prevention measures.
- If you have an important or challenging race or event, make sure that you train to the distance and pace of the event to help avoid cramp during your race.
- Remember that attention to fluid and electrolyte (mineral) levels is even more crucial during hot weather as you are more likely to become dehydrated and lose sodium through sweat losses.

Insight

The four minerals involved in muscular contraction are called the macro-minerals. Follow these dietary guidelines to ensure a balanced intake:

- Fill up on beans, pulses, green leafy vegetables, dairy produce, nuts and seeds for plenty of calcium and magnesium.
- Eat plenty of vegetables, fruit and juices for ample potassium.
- Cut back on salt. Most of us consume too much sodium in the form of salt and this can cause imbalances in the other macro-minerals. If you suffer with cramp regularly, try cutting back on salt by: not adding it to cooking; not using a salt pot; avoiding processed foods in tins, packets or jars as these usually have salt added for taste and as a preservative; and checking the label – low-salt products contain 0.1 g of sodium per 100 g. Your daily salt intake should not exceed six grams.

How can I treat it?

If you are in the middle of a run when you get a cramp, stop and gently stretch the offending muscle.

If you get cramp after your run...

1 *gently stretch the muscle*
2 *apply an ice pack*
3 *gently massage the area*
4 *replace lost fluid.*

Insight

Try an isotonic sports drink containing electrolytes during hot weather. Sports drinks usually contain electrolytes (sodium and potassium) and other minerals such as magnesium and calcium. When you consume a sports drink you are also replacing water and sugars (carbohydrate), so, if the cause of your cramp is dehydration, low blood sugar or lack of any of the macro-minerals, a sports drink before, during or after your run could help. Check out the differences between hypotonic, isotonic and hypertonic sports drinks in Chapter 6 'Food and drink on the run', to see which type would suit your running needs.

SIDE STITCH

Side stitch (also known as exercise-related transient abdominal pain) is a sharp pain that occurs at the bottom of the rib cage, usually on the right-hand side. Although it often occurs in new runners, it seems unrelated to how often or fast you run and at what level. There are still several theories as to what causes stitch.

Theory 1 – Side stitch is caused by a spasm in the diaphragm – the muscle that sits beneath your chest cavity and helps to control your breathing – and a possible cause is lack of a rhythmic breathing pattern.

However, although focusing on your breathing can reduce the occurrence of stitch and may alleviate it, this doesn't explain why lower-intensity exercise like horse riding causes it.

Theory 2 – Side stitch is caused by the stomach and liver pulling down on the diaphragm by the attaching ligaments. This is exaggerated by irregular jolting movements caused during running, and also if the stomach is full from recent food or drink.

However, stitches still occur in swimming where there is no similar jolting movement present, although the longitudinal rotation in swimming may pull on the diaphragm muscle.

Theory 3 – Side stitch is caused by lack of blood flow to the diaphragm.

However, our breathing pattern remains unaffected, and stitch occurs during lower-intensity activities such as horse riding which do not have a high circulatory requirement (but do have a jolting movement).

Theory 4 – Stitch might not be a spasm of the diaphragm, but may occur in the parietal peritoneum, a layer of connective tissue that envelops the abdominal cavity and related organs. The top part of it goes underneath the diaphragm, and eating or drinking prior to running would contribute to irritation of the parietal peritoneum.

Insight

Apparently, stitch seems more common in runners who exhale as the right foot hits the ground – this causes the liver to 'drop' more just as the diaphragm rises during exhalation, increasing the stretch and stress on the ligaments that attach the liver to the peritoneal cavity. So, next time you go running, consider how your stride and breathing go together, and see if exhaling as your left foot hits the ground reduces your stitch! It's possible that simply focusing on creating a regular breathing pattern and comfortable stride pattern will help anyway.

Whatever the cause or causes of side stitch, try these simple tips to help reduce the occurrence and deal with it effectively if you do get it during a run.

How to prevent a side stitch happening

▶ *Avoid eating or drinking sugary drinks such as cola or fruit juice before your run.*

▶ *Ensure optimum hydration as being dehydrated can increase the chance of muscle cramps (the diaphragm is a sheet of muscle).*

▶ *Make sure you warm up thoroughly, particularly in cold weather.*

▶ *Try to maintain a regular pace when you run, avoiding undue jolting of the internal organs.*

▶ *Keep breathing controlled and avoid shallow breathing.*

If you feel a side stitch coming on during a run...

1 *Focus on reducing any jolting movements in your running.*

2 *Reduce your pace slightly, place your right hand on your stomach and push upwards in an attempt to lift your liver and stomach, reducing the strain on the ligaments that are attached to the peritoneum or diaphragm.*

3 *Try to exhale when your left foot hits the floor.*

4 *Take deep, even breaths to allow the diaphragm to drop during the inhalation and reduce stress on the ligaments that are attached to the abdominal cavity.*

5 *Try taking deep breaths in through pursed lips and exhaling sharply.*

6 *Try pressing your fingers in directly where the stitch is.*

If your side stitch still brings you to a halt, try any of these methods...

7 *If you can, continue to walk, focus on your breathing and press your fingers into the area of the stitch.*

8 *Lift your right arm up and lean over to the left to stretch the diaphragm, holding for a few seconds and repeating on the other side.*

9 *Bend over forwards, contract the abdominal muscles, and press directly on the area of pain.*

Insight

When the diaphragm and surrounding tissues become irritated, pain may be felt in the tip of the right shoulder as this is an area that the phrenic nerve from the diaphragm serves. So, if you regularly experience a niggling pain in your shoulder that only ever appears whilst running, it may be stitch rather than a shoulder problem!

If you regularly experience side stitch whilst running, you may benefit from specific breathing and diaphragm 'training'. Many people breathe incorrectly or inadequately, and learning how to breathe properly can have a significant effect upon your running ability, as well as reducing stitch. You can do breathing exercises to retrain your respiratory muscles or invest in an inspiratory muscle trainer such as the POWERbreathe. For further information on this tool and for a range of breathing exercises, see the 'Taking it further' section at the end of this book.

RUNNER'S TROTS

Apart from being uncomfortable and potentially embarrassing, a desperate need to empty the bowel mid-run is so frustrating, as it's guaranteed to bring your run to a halt. 'Runner's trots' is often accompanied by cramps, flatulence or an uncomfortable, heavy feeling in the lower abdomen, all indicating that you need to find a toilet sooner rather than later!

This is caused by the jolting motion of running, which encourages the stool to move along in the large intestine. On a positive note, this helps to create more regular bowel movements and can prevent or reduce constipation, but it's not good news if it happens during a run. Try these tips to regulate normal bowel movements so that your bowel is empty when you run.

Tips to reduce the trots

▶ *Keep bowel movements regular with a high-fibre diet and ample water intake – this means filling up on cereals, beans and pulses, fruit and vegetables.*

- *Lack of water causes stools to become hard and dry; this makes them difficult to move along the large intestine and more material is stored in the bowel. With a backup of material waiting to be emptied from the bowel, the jolting movements during running aid peristalsis and get things moving. Remember that when you exercise you need more water to remain hydrated – drinking sufficient fluid will keep things moving along and enable you to empty your bowel every day.*

- *Try to empty your bowel before you go for a run. For some people, a cup of coffee can help to stimulate the bowel to empty, but make sure you get the timing right so it works before your run! This may work for you, and the caffeine will give your run an extra boost. For more information about the effects of caffeine, read the section on ergogenic aids in Chapter 6 'Food and drink on the run'.*

- *Check you do not have a food allergy or sensitivity, as this can cause 'dumping syndrome' when you suddenly have to empty the bowel. This is also common in those suffering from irritable bowel syndrome. You are advised to see your doctor or a qualified nutritional therapist if you suspect any of these complaints, but cutting out dairy produce and wheat is a good way to initially test for food intolerances – although there are many other culprits, these are two of the most common. Make sure you replace wheat products such as bread and pasta with other energy-rich foods such as rice, oats or quinoa, and replace calcium-rich dairy produce with enriched soya products, nuts, seeds and green leafy vegetables.*

Insight

If you still need help to create a regular habit and keep the bowel relatively empty after increasing your fibre and water intake, try adding psyllium husk fibre to juice. This natural fibre absorbs water and helps to create a regular bowel movement.

RUNNER'S NIPPLE

This occurs through clothing rubbing the nipples, usually during long runs when you're particularly sweaty. Some types of fabric are more likely to cause or exacerbate it: clothing that holds moisture (such as cotton T-shirts) or abrasive materials are common culprits.

Try these tips to stop it:

▶ *Wear running kit made from fabrics that wick moisture away from the skin.*
▶ *Apply Vaseline to the nipples (or any area of skin that has rubbed) to create a barrier between the fabric and your skin – this prevents chaffing and also reduces subsequent irritation once the area is inflamed.*
▶ *For really bad chaffing or for long runs and races, place plasters over the nipples.*

POST-RUNNING MUSCLE SORENESS

Delayed onset muscle soreness (DOMS) is common whenever you try a new activity, and also when you push the boundaries, running further or faster than usual. There is a big difference between muscle soreness and a muscular injury, and they feel completely different:

▶ *Muscle soreness is an ache that is usually worse if you use or stretch the muscle.*
▶ *A 'pulled' or injured muscle will give a more acute, sharper pain when the muscle is either used or stretched.*

Insight

It is a myth that the lactic acid formed during exercise such as running causes muscle soreness. Lactic acid is naturally removed from the muscle via the circulation long before delayed onset muscle soreness is felt.

What is muscle soreness?

Muscle soreness is the result of microscopic tears in the muscle fibres and a breakdown of the connective tissue that encapsulates the muscle fibres and attaches the muscle to bone. The good news is that after the muscle has recovered and rebuilt the damage, it is more resistant to the same level of exercise for approximately six weeks. This is one of the training adaptations that occur after any type of exercise, and explains why a new run will cause muscle soreness initially, but, once used to the new running speed, longer distance or more challenging terrain, the muscle adapts and you stop experiencing muscle soreness. However, you have to keep up with the new, harder runs to keep muscle soreness at bay – if you have a break and then return to a more difficult run, you will experience the soreness again. Although muscle soreness is a normal, natural phenomenon with regular, progressive exercise, there are things you can do to reduce and ease it.

Reducing the likelihood of muscle soreness

- ▶ *You are not going to stop increasing the distance or speed of your runs, but you may want to avoid these increases just before an important event or race when you can't afford to be stiff.*
- ▶ *Make your increases in speed or distance small ones so that the body has smaller adaptations to make.*
- ▶ *Running downhill puts greater strain on the muscles and connective tissue, and therefore often results in greater muscle soreness. Include downhill running in your training if you need to, but avoid it to reduce muscle soreness.*
- ▶ *Running at least once a week or fortnight at your peak speed and distance will help you to avoid muscle soreness as the body has already adapted to performing at this level.*
- ▶ *Applying ice (or jumping into an ice bath) will reduce inflammation and may reduce post-run muscle soreness.*
- ▶ *Make sure that you stretch and cool down gradually after a hard run to help the muscles begin the recovery phase.*
- ▶ *You need to allow the muscle to 'mend' if muscle soreness has set in: if you run again before it has healed and adapted, additional muscle soreness will occur.*
- ▶ *Regularly running will result in less post-running muscle soreness than running every now and then.*

Easing muscle soreness

Techniques for easing muscle soreness are mostly based upon massage and heat treatment:

▶ *Have a long, warm bath to help relax the muscles.*
▶ *Gently stretching the affected muscle will be difficult at first, but the muscle soreness will be eased afterwards.*
▶ *Sore muscles will be tender to the touch, but this will ease off during a massage, leaving the muscles feeling better afterwards.*

Sports massage

A regular sports massage has several benefits, including reducing the risk of injury:

✓ *It helps to relax muscles and release muscular tension.*
✓ *A good sports masseur/therapist will identify over-tight muscles or tender spots for you to be aware of, and apply remedial therapy.*
✓ *It increases blood flow to muscles, tendons and ligaments, enhancing nutrient delivery and aiding in elimination of post-exercise waste products from the muscles.*

- ✓ It may help to enhance the flexibility of muscles, tendons and bands of connective tissue such as the IT band.
- ✓ It creates an opportunity to focus on how your body is feeling, particularly any injury-prone areas, and provides valuable time for assessing how your running schedule is going.
- ✓ It creates a valuable relationship with your sports therapist or sports massage therapist – with regular massage, they will get to know your body and will let you know (if you don't feel it first) if any muscles or ligaments are tight or inflamed.
- ✓ It can provide an enjoyable psychological boost, maybe as a reward after so many runs, or as a balancing reward for the efforts your body makes during each run.

DIY MASSAGE

To massage yourself or supplement sports massages with some of your own massage therapy, invest in a foam roller. These lightweight yet sturdy rollers provide a deep and therapeutic massage for tight muscles and ligaments. One of the best exercises a runner can do is to massage the IT band:

Figure 8.1 IT band massage.

1 Lie on your side with the foam roller beneath your thigh.

2 *Take your upper body weight on your arm(s).*
3 *Slowly roll your body up and down the foam roller so that it rolls from the hip down to just below the knee and back again.*
4 *You can intensify the massage by relaxing more of your leg/body weight on to the foam roller.*
5 *Repeat the movement several times or until tenderness subsides.*
6 *Change sides.*

Running injuries

Approximately 65 per cent of runners sustain an injury that stops them from running for a while in any one year. However, most running injuries are overuse injuries – it seems that running is so addictive and enjoyable that we can't get enough of it once we start. Unfortunately, more is not always better!

A number of factors contribute to running injuries, such as whether you are a new or an experienced runner, where you choose to run, and the anatomy and physiology of your body, particularly your pelvis, legs and feet. The good news is that you can reduce the risk of most running injuries by following a sensible training programme and being aware of your body.

Factors that are under your control include:

▶ *your running schedule*
▶ *your choice of running shoe*
▶ *the type of surface you run on.*

You can't alter your anatomy, but you can do the following:

▶ *Buy running shoes that will help to create a good running gait.*
▶ *Use orthotics to compensate for uneven leg length and foot shape.*
▶ *Do remedial exercises and stretches to rebalance poor posture or alignment.*

So many common running injuries are easily preventable through more thorough warm-ups, correct running technique and simply listening to your body.

WHAT DO WE KNOW ABOUT RUNNING INJURIES?

A review of the causes of running injuries on www.medicinet.com/running mirrors the findings of several other reviews with the following results:

▶ *The most common injury site is the knee.*
▶ *Some older runners sustain more injuries, yet others experience less, so age is not a significant factor if your running form is good.*
▶ *Running only one day a week slightly increases injury risk.*
▶ *Running longer distances, up to 40 miles a week, does not incur more injuries and seems to reduce injury, but running more than 40 miles a week increases the risk of lower leg injuries, particularly in men.*
▶ *There appears to be no obvious association between the occurrence of injuries and stretching.*

> *Having previous injuries is a risk factor for running injuries. In addition, the older the running shoes the higher the risk of injury due to reduced support.*

Things that cause running injuries

Running injuries aren't only caused by suddenly pulling a muscle or twisting an ankle; in fact, many more running injuries are chronic rather than acute injuries and can be caused by:

▶ *lack of warm-up*
▶ *muscular imbalances*
▶ *poor running technique*
▶ *wearing badly fitting or worn-out running shoes.*

Acute injuries are usually sudden and significant, often caused by a fall, or by overstretching muscles, tendons or ligaments. A common example is spraining an ankle. Whilst these injuries often incur a reasonable amount of soft tissue damage, the cause and location of the injury are generally obvious and the injured part of the body can be treated and rested immediately.

Chronic injuries are those that have been ongoing for some time, possibly unknown and untreated. The problem with chronic injuries is that, as they have taken a while to build up, they often take a long time to heal and may have caused injury or imbalance in other areas whilst they have been present.

Insight

The length of time that an injury is present is a significant factor in the time needed for recovery. In other words, the longer you leave it, the worse it will become and the longer your running break will be.

Warming up before running has already been covered in Chapter 4 'Get set and go – from warm-up to cool-down', so you already know the benefits of warming up and how to do it. Many runners skip warming up as they feel they don't need to or have not got time for it, but even if you never warm up and have never had an injury whilst running yet, not warming up could be affecting your running form, which could cause a repetitive strain injury over a period of time.

Common running injuries

Regular, rather than intermittent, running initially reduces injury risk. However, as your weekly mileage increases, so does your likelihood of injury, but although spending more time running proportionately increases injury risk, this is usually as a result of poor technique or over-training. Two key factors to consider are:

1 *If you run with poor technique, the risk of injury increases with mileage.*
2 *The higher your mileage, the more you risk over-training.*

Insight

Although training for an endurance event such as a half marathon will entail running a reasonable amount of miles weekly, always bear in mind the following thought to keep yourself injury-free:

QUALITY OVER QUANTITY

You can always add additional runs to your regime, but you cannot take a run back after you have done one too many!

The following table shows the effect on injury incidence of running an increasing number of miles per week. Participants in this study were male, with an average age of 33.4 years; overall injury incidence was 37 per cent. Note the increasing number of injuries with rising mileage, particularly above 40 miles per week.

Miles per week	Number of runners	Injury incidence (% per year)
0–9	70	21.4
10–19	191	29.3
20–29	183	36.1
30–39	93	40.8
40–49	25	52
50+	31	71

Source: www.powerrunning.com

As you can see, there are a number of things you can do to help prevent running injuries, but, just in case, here's a rundown on some of the most common ones.

ILIOTIBIAL BAND INJURIES

These are very common in female runners and are caused by a lack of flexibility in a fibrous band of connective tissue (the iliotibial band) that runs down the outside of the leg from the hip to just below the knee. If any muscle or tendon is over-tight this affects the way that you run, and poor running form can lead to:

▶ *other muscular imbalances as they compensate for poor positioning*
▶ *poor footfall*
▶ *poor body alignment that can force a muscle, tendon or ligament into a position that puts it under stress, causing chronic muscle strains, tendonitis or ligament sprains, all with accompanying inflammation and discomfort.*

Think about how many steps you take during a run: any imbalance or incorrect movement is repeated over and over, going unnoticed for weeks, sometimes months, but creating a number of other problems as long as it continues.

How will I know if I have a tight iliotibial band?

If you have a tight iliotibial band you may experience pain or aching anywhere on the outside of the leg from just below the hip to the outside of the knee, or up and down the outside of the leg. Your running form may be affected and you may find the iliotibial stretches difficult. Try the stretch below to see if your IT band may cause you a problem, before it actually does...

How to see if your iliotibial band is tight

Lie on your side right on the edge of your bed facing inwards with one leg stacked on top of the other. Keeping your body still, allow the top leg to drop backwards and off the bed, and see if you can feel any tightness, particularly around the outer thigh area, or notice a difference between how far each leg drops down (swap sides of the bed to do the other leg). If one leg drops down much less than the other, this indicates a tighter IT band on this side. Stretch the IT band by getting into this position and holding it for a couple of minutes every day until the flexibility matches the other side.

The IT band is a long tendon that connects the tensor fascia lata (hip muscle) to the tibia (shin bone). It helps to stabilize the leg and if it is put under chronic stress such as being overworked because other stabilizing muscles are not strong enough, several things may happen:

▶ *You may strain the IT tendon.*
▶ *It may begin to pull away from the bone where it connects, causing pain in the hip or on the tibia.*
▶ *The tendon may rub on the bone creating inflammation and bursitis.*

What causes it?

Your stabilizing gluteal muscles may be weak if you have done little exercise to strengthen them in the past, and if these are weak, the IT band will have to work harder to stabilize the pelvis when you are running. Over time this can over-tighten it and cause any of the above IT band injuries.

Can I continue to run?

This depends on how tight your IT band is and whether it is affecting your running form – if it is painful to run or your running form is badly affected you will need to rest from running. Once the flexibility of your IT band has improved, you may find that you can do shorter and less intense runs whilst you work on full recovery and flexibility. Try slowing down your pace, inserting recovery walking intervals, and definitely reduce your running distance until you can run without any discomfort.

How can I treat it?

If a tight IT band is your only problem, you simply need to stretch it to increase the length and flexibility. Perform the IT band stretch at least twice a day, when you wake up and before you go to sleep, holding the stretch for a few minutes. You may also benefit from gently stretching the IT band before and after each run.

How long will it take to mend?

This will depend on:

- ▶ *how tight or short your IT band is*
- ▶ *whether there is something else (a muscle imbalance for example) causing the tightness; if so, this will also have to be treated*
- ▶ *how often and how long you spend stretching it.*

Prevention is better than cure

Perform the IT stretch regularly to prevent the muscle from becoming over-tight.

UNSUPPORTIVE GLUTEUS MEDIUS MUSCLES

The gluteus medius is the smaller gluteal muscle on the side of the hip, and one of its main roles is as a stabilizing muscle, particularly during running.

How will I know if my gluteal muscles are effective at stabilizing my pelvis?

Stand and look at your posture in a full-length mirror, and bend one knee so that your foot lifts off the floor. Your gluteal muscles should instantly contract to stabilize your pelvis: if you lose balance or see your hip drop on one side, the stabilizing muscles are not working as well as they might and you would benefit from some balance training.

What causes tight or unengaged gluteal muscles?

Stabilizing muscles such as the abdominals and gluteus medius need to be trained to be 'switched on' or 'engaged' – if they aren't regularly used in this way other muscles simply take over, and then the stabilizing muscles become weaker as they are used even less frequently.

Can I continue to run?

This depends on how tight or ineffective your gluteal muscles are and whether this is affecting your running form – if it is painful to run or your running form is badly affected, you will need to rest from running.

How can I treat it?

Stretch your gluteal muscles with the gluteal stretch in Chapter 4, and strengthen these muscles with the following single leg squat to enhance stabilization:

1 *Stand with weight distributed evenly and feet two inches apart.*
2 *Lift one foot just off the floor by slightly bending your knee.*
3 *Ensure that you don't compensate by taking your leg out to the side or to the back or front – keep it only just off the floor.*

4 *Engage your abdominal muscles to ensure core stability and slowly squat down as far as you can by bending your supporting leg.*

5 *Keep your hips and knees facing forwards and level (looking into a mirror whilst you do this exercise helps technique).*

6 *Slowly straighten up without locking the knee, and repeat 15–20 times.*

7 *Change legs and repeat the exercise.*

How long will it take to mend?

This will depend on:

▶ *how tight or weak your gluteus medius is*

▶ *whether there is something else (a muscle imbalance for example) causing the tightness – if so, this will also have to be treated*

▶ *how often and how long you spend stretching and/or strengthening it.*

KNEE PAIN

Knee pain is a common runner's complaint, although this can have many different causes, so 'knee pain' itself is a symptom of a specific injury or imbalance such as tendonitis or a tight IT band. For any type of knee pain, it is essential to find the cause – only when you treat this will the knee pains disappear. Common causes of knee pain include:

▶ *over-pronation (rolling-in) of the foot*

▶ *footfall not in line with knees and hips – e.g. feet turn outwards*

▶ *heavy heel strike increasing the impact on your knees as you run*

▶ *unbalanced or tight leg muscles.*

> **Insight**
>
> If you struggle with knee injuries or soreness, try to avoid downhill running until you have located and corrected the source of your knee problems, as this places even more pressure on your knees.

HEEL SPURS

A heel spur is a bony outgrowth of the heel bone caused by connective tissue inflammation. Heel spurs usually occur underneath the heel or where the tendons of the calf muscles insert into the calcaneus (heel bone), and often happen in conjunction with tendonitis of the Achilles tendon.

How will I know if I have heel spurs?
Heel spurs cause tenderness and pain underneath or at the back of the heel.

What causes it?
Inflammation may be caused by over-tight muscles or tendons, poor footwear or unbalanced footfall.

Can I continue to run?
Running is not recommended – it is likely to be painful and the inflammation and injury will become worse.

How can I treat it?
You need to reduce the inflammation and prevent it happening again. Follow these steps to get back running:

1 *Stop running if you feel pain or discomfort – this is a sign that you are doing more damage.*
2 *Ice the inflamed or painful area regularly.*
3 *For heel spurs underneath the heel, you may need to wear more cushioned everyday shoes or keep your weight off your feet as much as possible. Orthotic inserts can help to take the pressure off the heel and remove stress from a specific tendon or area of the foot to provide relief whilst the inflammation dies down and the tissues repair themselves.*
4 *For inflammation in the Achilles tendon it may be painful to wear flat shoes (which can stretch the tendon), so shoes with a slight heel that shorten the length of the tendon or inserts to lift your heel may help in the short term.*

However, if the tendon is short, this is a likely cause of the inflammation, and you need to gently stretch the calf muscles to increase the resting length of the Achilles tendon.

5 *Cortisone injections into the inflamed area may be suggested by your doctor or sports injury specialist in acute cases. Although this will reduce the inflammation, avoid running through the injury just because the pain or inflammation has been temporarily reduced (unless you have a race or event you have to take part in). A sports therapist or physiotherapist will assess the cause of the injury and provide advice on how to prevent it reoccurring.*

6 *You may need a new pair of running shoes with additional support or cushioning.*

How long will it take to mend?

Heel spurs may cause no symptoms at all, but if you are experiencing discomfort, try to remedy the cause and reduce the inflammation – the sooner you do this, the sooner you can get back out there! As with most injuries, recovery time will depend upon how bad the inflammation is. You may be able to continue with a lower-intensity running programme with orthotics reducing the stress whilst you remedy the cause.

Prevention is better than cure

▶ *Regularly stretch the calf muscles and Achilles tendon to avoid them becoming over-tight.*

▶ *Buy your running shoes from a specialist running shop to ensure a good fit and support for your foot shape and footfall.*

PLANTAR FASCIITIS

Plantar fasciitis is an inflammation of the band of tissue (ligament) that stretches underneath the sole of the foot, and is one of the most common causes of heel pain. This ligament supports the arch of the foot and connects the base of the toes to the heel, whilst a pad of fat cushions the heel and plantar fascia from impact when we run or walk.

How will I know if I have plantar fasciitis?

Your heels or the soles of your feet will feel tender either first thing in the morning when you first put your feet on the floor, or after standing on your feet for a while. You may experience sharp pain under the heel or a dull ache underneath the foot. If you sprain your plantar fascia, the bottom of your foot or your heel will be tender whenever you stand or walk.

What causes it?

Plantar fasciitis can be caused by anything that places a strain on the arch of the foot. Common causes are:

- *high arches of the foot*
- *flat feet*
- *over-pronation (your foot rolls inwards too much)*
- *standing, walking or running on hard surfaces*
- *excessive body weight*
- *tight Achilles tendon or tight calf muscles*
- *poor-fitting footwear*
- *frequent, high-intensity exercise such as running.*

This ligament often becomes inflamed when heel spurs occur and is sometimes called plantar heel spurs. It is important to try and discover the cause of the fasciitis to prevent it happening again – in particular:

- *check you have ample flexibility in your calf muscles and Achilles tendon – you should be able to take a reasonably large stride backwards to stretch these muscles and not feel tightness when you stretch*
- *check your footprint for over-pronation, flat feet or high arches (see Chapter 4 'Get set and go – from warm-up to cool-down') or check out your running gait (footfall) in a specialist running shop or with a podiatrist. Buy supportive running shoes and consider orthotics if necessary for your everyday shoes to prevent inward rolling and provide extra support*
- *lose weight if you are overweight*
- *avoid standing or running on hard surfaces.*

Can I continue to run?

No – the inflammation and injury will just become worse.

How can I treat it?

Follow the following guidelines initially and, if the pain continues, see a physiotherapist or sports therapist for advice and a definite diagnosis.

▶ *Stop running!*
▶ *Rest your feet as much as you can – avoid walking or standing for long periods of time.*
▶ *Keep off hard surfaces such as concrete pavements.*
▶ *Ice your heel or the bottom of your foot to reduce inflammation.*
▶ *Wear shoes with good arch support and cushioning.*
▶ *Avoid walking around bare foot.*
▶ *Consider inserting orthotics in your shoes to provide extra cushioning, support the arch of your foot and remove tension from the Achilles tendon.*
▶ *Gently massage the sole of the foot several times daily to release tension in the ligament and increase circulation.*
▶ *Perform gentle calf stretches several times a day (see the stretches in Chapter 4 'Get set and go – from warm-up to cool-down'). You can also stretch the calves by standing on a step, placing the toes of one foot on the edge of the step, and allowing the heel to drop downwards.*

Insight

To stretch the calf muscles and the Achilles tendon adequately, bear these guidelines in mind:

▶ *You should not feel any pain when you stretch*
▶ *Ease into each position slowly and stop when you feel a stretch in the muscle or tendon*
▶ *Relax into this stretch and hold for 30 seconds*
▶ *Now see if you can stretch a little further and hold again.*

Exercises for the plantar fascia

Try these exercises to ease plantar fasciitis, particularly first thing in the morning or after being on your feet for a long time. Doing these exercises every day will also help to prevent the condition recurring as they strengthen the foot muscles that support the arch of the foot and increase the flexibility of the plantar fascia.

▶ *Before you get out of bed, flex your foot up and down ten times slowly. Each time you bring the toes up towards you, you will feel a stretch underneath your foot – hold this position for ten seconds.*
▶ *Place a rolled towel beneath your foot, holding the ends and keeping your leg straight. Pull both ends of the towel towards you, stretching the bottom of the foot and calf muscles. Hold this for 20–30 seconds.*
▶ *Whilst seated, roll a tennis ball underneath the arch of your foot. Progress to doing this whilst standing when you can.*
▶ *Try picking things up with your toes! This provides a workout for the foot muscles that they don't often get.*

How long will it take to mend?
As with all injuries, this will depend upon the severity of the fasciitis, how long you have had it, and how much remedial exercise you can do to enhance recovery. Plantar fasciitis normally develops over a long period of time, so it usually takes a few weeks or even months to fully heal.

Prevention is better than cure
▶ *Do the exercises above to strengthen and stretch the foot muscles and ligaments.*
▶ *Wear shoes with good arch support and cushioning.*
▶ *Avoid running or walking long distances on very hard surfaces – run on dirt tracks or tarmac rather than concrete pavements, or at least vary your running terrain.*

ANKLE SPRAINS

Ankle sprains are one of the most common musculoskeletal injuries, and are caused by a sudden overstretching and tearing in the ankle ligaments, usually when we twist or 'go over' on an ankle. A ligament tear can be partial or complete, and this dictates the level of the injury and how long it will take to mend. An ankle sprain is more likely if you have previously sprained your ankle, as this will lengthen and weaken the ligament and leave your ankle joint with less stability than before, predisposing you to further injuries.

How will I know if I have sprained my ankle ligament?

You will probably be aware of twisting your ankle during a run, but you could incur a small strain without realizing it and just feel some tenderness later on. Your ankle may become swollen and reddened, could be tender to the touch, and the ankle joint will feel unsupportive or wobbly.

A partial tear means that the ligament is still attached across the ankle joint and continues to provide some stability; a complete tear through a ligament will provide no stability for the ankle joint. Although the amount of pain may not directly relate to the ligament damage, a complete ligament tear will generally be more painful when the foot is moved than a partial tear. If you have a bad ankle sprain, you may need an X-ray to evaluate the damage as ligaments attached to bone sometimes pull a piece of bone away as they tear.

What causes it?

An ankle sprain is usually caused by sudden movements, changes in direction or uneven ground tipping the foot over. A previous sprain may weaken the ankle joint so that it is less supported than normal, and this may cause further ankle sprains.

Can I continue to run?

This will depend on the severity of the sprain – a small sprain may be fine during short runs, as long as the ankle joint isn't tested by uneven road surfaces and you have plenty of ankle support. However, the last thing you want to do is turn a small sprain into a bigger injury by going over on your ankle whilst the ligaments are weak, so the best advice is to rest it until it is mended.

How can I treat it?

Ankle sprains should be iced and rested, and keeping the foot up can help to reduce inflammation and swelling. An elastic bandage can also help to reduce inflammation through compression around the injured area. Depending on the severity of the sprain, you may need to stay off your feet for a day or two. If your sprain is any worse than this, an X-ray, crutches, a plaster cast or surgery may be required.

Insight

Remember that ligaments support joints, and if your ankle ligament has been partially torn, it will be unable to provide full support for your ankle joint. For a few days after a sprain, consider wearing a support bandage around the ankle, avoid high-impact activities such as running and be careful of uneven terrain. Wearing a pair of hiking boots or trainers with ankle support may be helpful until the ligament mends.

How long will it take to mend?

This will depend upon whether you suffer a partial or complete tear of the ankle ligament. Partial tears may take from a few days to weeks to heal, but for complete tears requiring plaster casts you'd better hang up your running shoes for a while...

Prevention is better than cure

Although wearing ankle supports such as a neoprene bandage can help to stabilize the ankle joint, the best thing to do is strengthen the muscles and ligaments around the ankle as follows:

▶ *Although running off-road on uneven ground can cause a twisted ankle if you don't watch where your feet are going, uneven terrain will help to strengthen the ankle joint. Every time the muscles and ligaments in the foot are 'tested' on uneven ground, this works and strengthens the parts of the foot that are responsible for preventing an ankle sprain.*
▶ *Invest in a wobble board! Balance training has increased in popularity over the last few years. It is a functional exercise where the muscles, tendons and ligaments are exercised in*

the same way that they function on a daily basis, making them better at 'doing their job'. Balance training is also great for strengthening core muscles (abdominals and lower back muscles) and stabilizing muscles that are often weak and contribute to poor running form and injuries.

TENDONITIS

Tendons are part of the connective tissue that encapsulates the muscle and then attaches the muscle to bone. Tendonitis is inflammation of the tendon and can occur in any tendon in the body, although it is more common in leg and foot tendons in runners, such as the Achilles tendon or just below the patella (knee bone) where the quadriceps muscles insert into the tibia (shin).

How will I know if I have tendonitis?
You may experience either sharp pains in the localized area (in the Achilles tendon for example), or a 'niggling' pain or ache whilst running or between runs. There may be inflammation and tenderness in the area, and the pain may be worse when the muscle that the tendon is attached to is used.

What causes it?
You may experience tendonitis after an acute injury such as a muscle strain or torn tendon, or cause tendonitis over a period of time through poor running form or incorrect body alignment whilst you run. It is a common overuse injury.

Can I continue to run?
This depends on the severity of the tendonitis, but it is best to avoid running whilst you are suffering from any injury or trauma in the areas directly affected by running. If it is likely that running has caused the tendonitis, continuing will prolong the injury and potentially make it worse.

How can I treat it?
▶ *Rest the area and apply ice, and elevate it if it is a lower extremity such as the ankle or knee.*

- Avoid using the muscles and joints in that area as much as possible and try to identify the cause of the tendonitis, especially if it has been caused by repetitive movement rather than an acute injury.
- You may require the help of a physiotherapist, sports therapist or podiatrist to analyse your running gait or pinpoint muscular imbalances to avoid creating the same problem when you return to your running.

Insight

If you experience any muscle, tendon or ligament injuries through frequent running as opposed to an acute injury...

- Have you been running too frequently? Simply reducing your running mileage may be all you need to do to avoid further similar injuries.
- Do you warm up properly before running? You may be placing muscles, tendons and ligaments under more stress than is necessary.
- Do you feel tightness in certain areas and, if so, do you stretch those muscles? Over-tight and unbalanced muscles is a key cause of tendonitis, particularly tight calf muscles and over-tight iliotibial bands.
- Have you analysed your posture, body alignment and running gait? If not, have a running partner, fitness coach or friends watch you run and give you feedback on your body positioning. If in doubt, consult a specialist for some expert advice.

How long will it take to mend?
As with all injuries, this will depend upon the severity of the tendonitis, how long you have had it, and how much rest you give the muscle and tendon.

Prevention is better than cure
- Warm up thoroughly before running to avoid acute injuries such as torn muscles or tendons, especially if you are doing sprint training or planning a fast-paced run.

- *Regularly stretch all muscles to maintain muscle length and enhance muscular balance, particularly those used repeatedly during a run.*
- *Be aware of your technique and body alignment whilst you run: tendonitis is often caused over a period of time by bad positioning or form whilst running.*

SHIN SPLINTS

This is a fairly generic term for injuries occurring on or around the tibia or shin bone, including anterior shin splints, compartment syndrome and medial tibial stress syndrome. Although all these conditions are different, they all affect the same area – hence they were previously collectively termed as shin splints and this is the familiar term used here. However, for any ongoing problem it is essential to seek professional advice and obtain an accurate diagnosis of the exact nature of the injury.

Shin splints are often referred to as an overuse injury and usually occur in those frequently running or doing high-impact activities such as aerobics. Shin splints appear to be the result of injury to the tendons and tissues in this part of the leg, but severe cases can also involve stress fractures in the tibia (shin bone).

How will I know if I have shin splints?
Shin splints cause pain along the length of the shin bone (tibia), which may be felt upon impact during running, or just walking around during the day. The sensation is usually a dull ache, although with continued trauma to the area the pain may become more acute. The area may also feel tender to the touch, as if it has been bruised.

What causes it?
There are several possible causes of shin splints.

- *Some runners experience shin splints only when running in old running shoes, and the problem goes away when these are replaced with new running shoes with more cushioning.*

Not having enough shoe cushioning or wearing the wrong type of shoe for your footfall can increase the impact up the tibia and on the muscles and tendons attached: purchasing a good pair of new running shoes may be all you need to do.

▶ Running on hard ground such as concrete increases the impact forces on the lower leg and can be a causative factor.

▶ An increase in running distance, pace or frequency can all contribute to shin splints due to the increased work that the muscles at the front of the lower leg have to do, which can result in inflammation.

▶ Excessive pronation (where the foot rolls inwards too much) can exacerbate shin splints.

Insight

Depending upon how much you weigh (the more you weigh, the quicker your shoes will wear out) and what type of surface you regularly run on, the average pair of running shoes will last for approximately 300–500 miles, or about six months if you are running several times a week.

Do the following checks after you've clocked 300 miles...

▶ Check to see if there is an imprint of your foot on the insole.
▶ Check at the front of the shoe to see if the sole is coming away from the top of the shoe.
▶ Check the sides and the bottom of your shoe for cracking.
▶ Hold your running shoe at the heel and halfway down the forefoot and twist it – if it twists easily and gives way, the mid-sole is worn and you need to replace your running shoes.

You could also take your existing shoes to a running shoe shop and check how new shoes feel in comparison – if they feel much more comfortable, more cushioned or more supportive than your current shoes, it's likely you need a new pair.

Can I continue to run?

Continuing with your current running programme is not recommended – the shin splints will just worsen as trauma to the bone, muscle and tendons continues. As with all injuries, stopping now will enable the tissues to heal more quickly and effectively, allowing you to return to running sooner and with less risk of repeated symptoms.

How can I treat it?

▶ *If you can, give impact activities such as running a rest whilst the injury heals and enjoy non-impact exercise such as cycling or swimming to maintain cardiovascular fitness.*

▶ *Stop running or at least reduce your running by 50 per cent.*

▶ *Try to identify the cause – do you need new shoes, are you running too much or are you running on a hard surface such as concrete pavements?*

▶ *If you continue to run, choose runs with a softer terrain – dirt paths or tracks, fields, hard sand, or consider some treadmill running for a while, as treadmill belts have considerably more 'give' than roads or pavements.*

▶ *Choose more level routes rather than tackling hills – the angle of incline puts more strain on the muscles and tendons involved.*

▶ *Ice the area to reduce inflammation and swelling.*

▶ *Gently stretch and strengthen the muscles in the lower leg. Calf stretches are shown in Chapter 4 'Get set and go – from warm-up to cool-down', and the tibialis anterior at the front of the shin is stretched by pointing the toes downwards.*

▶ *If you aren't sure of the diagnosis or whether your running gait (footfall) may be to blame, get professional advice.*

How long will it take to mend?

As with any injury, the longer you have had it, the longer it will take to fix. If you stop running as soon as you experience any shin pain and identify – and fix – the cause, you may be able to get back on the road within two weeks.

Insight

After a break from running, don't go back to your normal pace and distance. Gradually increase the distance over the first month, and then consider increasing the pace. If you begin running again too soon and are still experiencing pain, stop immediately and give yourself more recovery time.

Prevention is better than cure

▶ *Replace your running shoes in good time.*
▶ *Buy running shoes that help to prevent excessive pronation (where the foot rolls inwards), if this describes your footfall.*
▶ *Vary your running routes to avoid running on hard concrete pavements too often.*

_____

Preventing running injuries

Some injuries may cause you to adjust your running regime rather than have to stop altogether. This is more likely if...

▶ *the injury or sensation is new*
▶ *the injury or sensation is more of an awareness than a pain*
▶ *you are a seasoned runner.*

If you have been doing a fair amount of running, just easing back may be all you need to do, and there are several options open to you.

REDUCING YOUR RUNNING INTENSITY

There are a number of ways you can do this:

▶ *Reduce the number of runs that you do.*
▶ *Reduce the distance that you run.*
▶ *Reduce your running pace.*
▶ *Allow more rest time between runs.*

- ▶ *Stick to flat, easy routes.*
- ▶ *Reduce the intensity with intervals of slow jogging or recovery walking.*
- ▶ *Mix running with alternative types of exercise (cross-train).*

See Chapter 7 'Running to suit you' for cross-training exercise options and ideas. Unfortunately, many common running injuries will prevent you from running – maybe not at first, as many runners wrongly 'carry' injuries and continue to run, but the longer you carry on running, the worse the injury will become and the longer your rest from running will have to be in the long run. Continuing to exercise with other types of activity can help keep you fit and motivated, and make you less likely to begin running again too soon.

Insight

If you become injured, stop running and let the injury heal. This is the quickest way back to your regular running regime. Get to know a local sports therapist or physiotherapist who can provide you with good advice when you need it. If you know someone who can help before you sustain an injury, you are more likely to seek professional advice when you need it.

Exercises to help injury prevention

To help prevent common running injuries, try doing these strengthening exercises two to three times weekly, maybe after a run or whilst watching television!

Help prevent knee and hip injuries

Prevention of these injuries involves strengthening and stabilizing gluteal muscles.

1 *Lie on your side with hips bent forward at 45 degrees, knees bent at approximately 45 degrees and feet stacked one on top of the other.*
2 *Slowly rotate your top leg backwards, lifting your leg a few inches and rotating your knee up towards the ceiling, whilst*

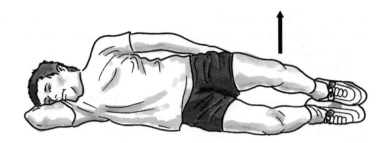

Figure 8.2 Knee and hip injury prevention.

*keeping the ankles together. Then lower back to the starting
point and repeat 15–20 times.*

3 *Keep the rest of your body still and hips facing forwards, not
allowing yourself to roll backwards.*

4 *Change legs and repeat.*

Help prevent sprained ankles and shin splints

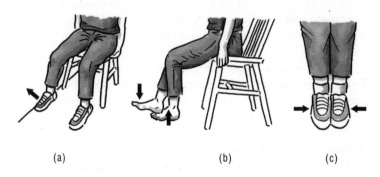

(a)   (b)   (c)

Figure 8.3 Sprained ankle and shin splint prevention.

Exercise (a)

1 *Sit on a chair and push the side of your foot against the wall
for 3–5 seconds, then relax.*

2 *Repeat 10–15 times on each leg.*

Exercise (b)

1 *Sit on a chair and place the heel of one foot on top of the other foot.*
2 *Push down with the top foot whilst pushing up with the bottom foot.*

Exercise (c)

1 *Sit down and push your feet inwards against each other.*
2 *Hold for 3–5 seconds and repeat.*

Top ten tips for injury prevention

Injuries can affect running form significantly. Our muscles work in conjunction with one another, so, if one muscle or movement is slightly 'off', it causes a knock-on effect onto other muscles, joints and connective tissue. Often, an injury in one part of the body may have been caused by an imbalance in an entirely different area. Whereas you can help to prevent injuries by concentrating on alignment and balance in each part of the body, it may be very difficult for you to try and figure out what has caused an injury and how to put it right. Unless the cause of an injury is obvious, seek professional advice sooner rather than later, as you will only exacerbate the problem by continuing to run or trying to fix it yourself. There are, however, ways in which you can be proactive to help avoid injury. Here are ten tips:

1 *Always warm up thoroughly, particularly in cold weather or for more intense training sessions.*
2 *Invest in a good pair of running shoes and replace them before you notice that you need to whilst running. If you know what your weekly average mileage is, work out how many months before you run 300–500 miles and make a note in your running log or on your calendar to check your running shoes to help prevent shin splints and heel spurs.*

3 *Concentrate on your posture and body alignment whilst running – every few minutes, refocus your mind to do a body check, and make sure shoulders are relaxed, abdominals engaged, hips and knees are in alignment. This helps to prevent chronic injuries through poor alignment or running form. If your posture or body alignment is poor, either do some muscular rebalancing exercises at the gym with the help of a qualified instructor, or see a sports therapist.*

4 *Check your running gait. You can get a running partner or friend to watch you run and tell you what your footfall is like, or maybe do a run on a treadmill in front of a mirror so you can see your gait for yourself. Better still, seek expert advice at a specialist running shop, or from a podiatrist or sports therapist, or see the 'Taking it further' section for gait analysis specialists across the UK. Once you understand what your footfall pattern is, invest in the right type of running shoes.*

5 *Don't try to progress too quickly – increase your running distance or running time by no more than 10 per cent each week.*

6 *Alter the type of terrain you run on, and have a menu of runs that you choose from. Running on the same surfaces several times a week is more likely to create problems than if you vary your runs. Be particularly aware of running on concrete pavements, soft sand or sloping surfaces (cambered roads); try to run routes the opposite way round, and vary distances too.*

7 *Make sure you have rest days from running (and other high-impact exercise) so that you don't overdo it – research indicates that high-impact activity done more than four times weekly results in more overuse injuries. Failing to give your body time to repair after a run is asking for trouble. You will also be physically and mentally tired, which makes you more likely to trip or twist an ankle.*

8 *Refuelling is important too – without enough fluid and carbohydrate in your diet and rest days to allow your glycogen stores to be replenished, you will be running with*

(Contd)

> *reduced energy levels, increasing the likelihood of poor running form and injuries.*
>
> 9 *Do not try to run through existing injuries or medical problems – get them checked out by an expert and take their advice. Running with one injury is likely to cause another.*
>
> 10 *Going back to running too soon without allowing an injury to fully heal can undo weeks of rest and put you back even further. Make sure that you return at a slower pace and reduce mileage as well – don't expect to run what you used to.*

Does my condition prevent me from running?

If you are already a runner, the last thing you want is for something to get in the way of your runs. If you have a known existing condition and have been running with no problems, then you will probably continue to do so, but when something new comes up, it can stop you in your tracks. The good news is that for the vast majority of health conditions, running is beneficial. It improves cardiovascular health and promotes circulation; it helps with weight control and aids blood glucose regulation, and it enhances lung efficiency and respiratory health.

However, running is an intense form of exercise, so if you are new to running but have an existing health condition, it's worth having a pre-run check-up with your doctor before you begin. Once you have the go-ahead to begin running, make use of the guidelines and advice for several common health conditions below.

Asthma

Although having asthma may put you off running, regular running will improve the efficiency of your lungs and respiratory system, reducing the occurrence and severity of attacks.

THINGS TO DO IF YOU HAVE ASTHMA AND RUN

▶ *Take your inhaler or medication with you.*
▶ *Run with a running partner or let others know where you are running.*
▶ *Try not to go too far off the beaten track in case you do have a severe attack.*
▶ *Avoid cold weather as this closes up the airways and makes an asthma attack more likely.*

NASAL STRIPS

You may have seen athletes and runners wearing nasal strips during events such as marathons. The idea of these is to increase the amount of oxygen taken in to optimize performance. Although many runners report enhanced performance when wearing these strips, scientific trials show no measurable benefits. However, the amount of air taken in through the nose can be increased by 10–25 per cent – if you have exercise-induced asthma, this may be worth trying.

Insight

Nasal breathing has been shown to decrease the severity of exercise-induced asthma, so increasing the amount of air you can breathe in through the nose may be of benefit when you run. One pilot study involved 12 runners running for six minutes, once with a placebo (dummy nose strip) and once wearing nasal strips. Five of the 12 subjects had a decreased asthma response when wearing the nasal strip, suggesting that improved nasal breathing may decrease exercise-induced asthma.

Hay fever

Hay fever is an allergic reaction to tree, plant or grass pollen, and typically creates symptoms such as sneezing, an itchy, runny nose

and itchy eyes. If you can run through your hay fever, there's no
reason not to, and there are several things that might improve both
your symptoms and therefore your quality of running throughout
summer.

THINGS TO DO IF YOU SUFFER WITH HAY FEVER

▶ *Keep the windows closed overnight to avoid too much pollen
drifting in to the house.*
▶ *Reducing the amount of house dust around can alleviate
symptoms, so change the bed sheets, dust and vacuum
regularly.*
▶ *Most pollen is released early morning, so this may not be the
best time to run.*
▶ *Check weather reports and avoid running when there is a high
pollen count.*
▶ *Stick to road running and stay away from fields, especially if
the pollen count is high.*
▶ *Take hay fever medication as required – you may find it
useful to take the medication before the hay fever season
begins so that as little running as possible is affected by your
symptoms.*
▶ *Using a nasal spray just before you go out can help to reduce
symptoms during your run.*
▶ *Check with your doctor or chemist which types of medication
are best to take in conjunction with running, as some of the
decongestants can increase heart rate.*
▶ *Even better, try a naturopathic, homeopathic or herbal remedy
to help reduce your hay fever.*
▶ *Jump into the shower as soon as you finish your run –
showering pollen off your face and body or just rinsing your
face thoroughly can help to reduce the after-effects of
a summer run.*

Insight

If you are a fitness fanatic, then the last thing you want
to do is load up on hay fever medication. Why not try a
naturopathic remedy instead?

> ▶ *Fill up on foods with an anti-inflammatory effect – eat onions, fish, linseeds and linseed oil every day.*
> ▶ *Try a herbal remedy – Bromelain has an effective anti-inflammatory effect.*

Pregnancy – during and after

Taking up running during pregnancy is not an ideal time to begin, but many women who already run continue a number of months into the pregnancy, and women who exercised prior to pregnancy are able to cope with higher-intensity exercise during pregnancy than those who did not exercise before.

The benefits of continuing with regular running through pregnancy are:

- ✓ *continued fitness*
- ✓ *better weight control throughout and after pregnancy*
- ✓ *stress relief*
- ✓ *Many women have an easier pregnancy*
- ✓ *Many women have a better recovery after delivery*
- ✓ *Healthier babies with a higher birth weight.*

Continuing regular exercise can also help to alleviate problems that commonly accompany pregnancy such as elevated blood pressure or constipation. However, there are some physiological changes that take place during pregnancy that make running more difficult and create specific considerations.

WEIGHT GAIN DURING PREGNANCY

Although weight gain should be mostly in the third trimester, you will notice that any gain in weight makes running more difficult, as you have to carry your body weight with you on your run. Women often find it becomes uncomfortable to run once a sizeable bump has begun to form, although supportive cycle shorts or maternity belts can help.

Other considerations when running with extra weight include:

▶ *Some of the extra weight is due to increases in breast tissue, so you may need to invest in a larger or more supportive running bra.*
▶ *The extra weight may mean that you have to slow down a little, reduce your run by a couple of miles, or use recovery walking to help you get your breath back.*

The great thing about running is that transition from your normal routine is easy; simply gradually decrease the intensity, distance and time of your runs right through to power-walking in the final trimester. It's just like following a progressive running programme in reverse. You may need to swap hilly routes for more steady runs as well, and think about your running terrain, as your balance will also begin to be affected.

CHANGES IN YOUR CENTRE OF GRAVITY

As most of the weight gained during pregnancy is at the front of the body, this moves your centre of gravity forwards and affects your balance. This is one of the main reasons why high-impact activities such as running or aerobics classes are not advised during pregnancy due to the risk of falling over.

For this reason, you may find that you are less steady on your feet as your pregnancy progresses, and your run may need to be replaced with a low-impact power-walk. Low-impact activities always have one foot on the ground, making it easier to maintain your balance.

HORMONAL CHANGES

A hormone called relaxin is released during pregnancy, more so during the latter half. This hormone softens the baby's and your ligaments in preparation for delivery, but the increased flexibility around joints also means lower joint stability and a higher risk of injuries such as a sprained ankle. This is a further reason to choose your running route carefully and consider dropping from running to walking.

Whilst relaxin is circulating in your body, you also need to take care not to overstretch, as joints and ligaments can be damaged from overstretching at this time.

INCREASED BODY TEMPERATURE

Although some women do continue to run throughout pregnancy, one aspect of high-intensity exercise that can be detrimental to the foetus is elevated foetal temperature – as your body temperature increases, so does that of the baby. This is another reason why health and fitness professionals usually advise reducing exercise intensity during pregnancy. Wear comfortable, loose-fitting clothes to help keep you cool, stay well hydrated, and avoid running on hot days as your body temperature will automatically be higher than normal.

There are a number of ways to reduce intensity – just take your pick from the following:

▶ *Reduce your running pace to a slower speed.*
▶ *Introduce intervals of slower jogs or recovery walking.*

- *Avoid hill runs and stick to the flat.*
- *Reduce the distance of your running routes.*

Running will feel more difficult than normal as heart rate increases during pregnancy, so there's not much point using a heart rate monitor to assess fitness levels.

Insight

As the extra weight begins to press on your bladder, you might want to plan a new route which keeps you closer to home in case you need the toilet mid-run. This also gives you an option to cut your run short if you become tired. Doing two loops of your 'block' might work better than a route that is the same distance but takes you further afield.

IMPORTANT!

Don't run during pregnancy if:

- this is your first pregnancy
- you are expecting twins or more
- you are in the first trimester
- you have previously had miscarriages, premature babies or other problems
- you experience bleeding or any other discomfort.

If in doubt, check with your doctor before you go out running.

POST-PREGNANCY

Women vary greatly in how quickly they are able to get back to running or regular exercise, which is partly dependant upon the delivery. Doctors and fitness professionals usually advise that you should have your six-week, post-delivery check-up before starting back, although many women begin exercise, including running, much sooner.

Although running is 'me time' for many, you may not have a babysitter or want to be parted from your new arrival, so a baby jogger or baby stroller may be a consideration. This is a pram with large, sturdy wheels that you can run or power-walk with, enabling you to get back into your routine. However, if possible, try one before you make a purchase, as holding on to handlebars in front of you may not suit your running form at all.

Excess body weight

Although running is one of the most effective exercises for weight loss, it is also one of the most difficult if you are overweight. As running is a weight-bearing exercise, the lighter you are, the easier it is... and the heavier you are, the harder it is. Because it is more difficult to exercise with a high body weight, your heart rate and perceived exertion (how difficult it is) are both elevated.

However, the benefit of weighing more whilst doing weight-bearing exercise is that you will be using up much more energy. Running uses more calories than most other forms of exercise, so, even if you have to begin by doing mostly walking with brief interludes of jogging, it is certainly worth doing. As you lose weight you will find it easier to run and, in conjunction with increased fitness levels, you should progress reasonably quickly.

If you are more than two stones heavier than you should be, it is worth having a health check-up with your doctor before you begin, as obesity is linked with heart disease and diabetes. However, the risk of heart disease and diabetes is reduced through activities such as regular running, and it is likely that your doctor will recommend regular exercise. Having health parameters that will alter as you become fitter can create useful goals in addition to those you set yourself when you begin running. It is exceptionally motivating to see weight and body-fat levels reduce whilst blood pressure, cholesterol and resting blood sugar levels are also dropping.

The other main consideration of extra body weight is the pressure that running may have on your joints. You may initially find that it is just too difficult or uncomfortable to try and jog. If this is the case, simply follow the pre-run programme below to help you reduce your body weight and strengthen hip, knee and ankle joints in preparation for your running programme.

PRE-RUN EXERCISE PROGRAMMES

Your pre-run programme could also include non-weight-bearing exercises such as swimming, cycling or rowing to help prepare your body for running, also enjoying the following benefits:

- ✓ *increased cardiovascular fitness*
- ✓ *reduced body weight*
- ✓ *stronger joints*
- ✓ *a regular exercise habit.*

Weight training will also help, as it increases lean tissue (which elevates metabolic rate, increasing calorie expenditure and maximizing weight loss) and strengthens joints. However, if you can walk, a power-walking programme as shown below is a great pre-run programme as it offers several other benefits:

- ✓ *You get into the habit of walking around your running routes*
- ✓ *You can build up the habit of going out for a walk, which you will then progress into a run*
- ✓ *You can inject a few yards of jogging throughout your walk*
- ✓ *You can go hiking and do hill walks to increase intensity*
- ✓ *Walking is weight-bearing exercise, and it specifically helps to strengthen bones and joints in the lower limbs in preparation for running.*

Pre-run power-walking programme 1

	MON	TUES	WED	THURS	FRI	SAT	SUN
WEEK 1	20-min walk	Rest day	20-min walk	Rest day	20-min walk	Rest day	30-min walk
WEEK 2	25-min walk	Rest day	25-min walk	Rest day	25-min walk	Rest day	40-min walk
WEEK 3	30-min walk	Rest day	30-min walk	Rest day	30-min walk	Rest day	50-min walk
WEEK 4	40-min walk	Rest day	40-min walk	Rest day	40-min walk	Rest day	1 hour walk

(Contd)

	MON	TUES	WED	THURS	FRI	SAT	SUN
WEEK 5	40-min fast walk	Rest day	40-min fast walk	Rest day	40-min fast walk	Rest day	1-hour + walk
WEEK 6	40-min fast walk	Rest day	40-min fast walk	Rest day	40-min fast walk	Rest day	1-hour + walk

You can continue to progress this programme by doing longer walks, doing more walks, adding hill walks or doing faster walks. Once you can add 30 seconds of slow jogging every few minutes in your walk, you are ready for the next programme which introduces you to jogging.

Pre-run power-walking programme 2

	MON	TUES	WED	THURS	FRI	SAT	SUN
WEEK 1	Walk 5 mins Jog 0.5 mins 4 times	Rest day	Walk 5 mins Jog 0.5 mins 4 times	Rest day	Walk 5 mins Jog 0.5 mins 4 times	Rest day	Walk 5 mins Jog 0.5 mins 4 times
TIME	22 mins		22 mins		22 mins		22 mins
WEEK 2	Walk 4 mins Jog 0.5 mins 5 times	Rest day	Walk 4 mins Jog 0.5 mins 5 times	Rest day	Walk 4 mins Jog 0.5 mins 5 times	Rest day	Walk 4 mins Jog 0.5 mins 5 times
TIME	22.5 mins		22.5 mins		22.5 mins		22.5 mins

	MON	TUES	WED	THURS	FRI	SAT	SUN
WEEK 3	Walk 3 mins Jog 0.5 mins 6 times	Rest day	Walk 3 mins Jog 0.5 mins 6 times	Rest day	Walk 3 mins Jog 0.5 mins 6 times	Rest day	Walk or cycle 1 hour+
TIME	20 mins		20 mins		20 mins		
WEEK 4	Walk 3 mins Jog 1 min 5 times	Rest day	Walk 3 mins Jog 1 min 5 times	Rest day	Walk 3 mins Jog 1 min 5 times	Rest day	Walk or cycle 1 hour+
TIME	20 mins		20 mins		20 mins		
WEEK 5	Walk 3 mins Jog 1.5 mins 5 times	Rest day	Walk 3 mins Jog 1.5 mins 5 times	Rest day	Walk 3 mins Jog 1.5 mins 5 times	Rest day	Walk or cycle 1 hour+
TIME	22.5 mins		22.5 mins		22.5 mins		
WEEK 6	Walk 3 mins Jog 2 mins 5 times	Rest day	Walk 3 mins Jog 2 mins 5 times	Rest day	Walk 3 mins Jog 2 mins 5 times	Rest day	Walk or cycle 1 hour+
TIME	25 mins		25 mins		25 mins		

The next stage

After completion of these two six-week programmes, the latter one introducing you to jogging with recovery walking, you should have lost weight, be significantly fitter and have stronger muscles and joints. If you feel ready, you can now progress onto the programme for beginner runners in Chapter 4 'Get set and go – from warm-up to cool-down'. This programme continues on where the pre-run programme 2 ends, but you can always repeat a week or two if you aren't ready for the next level.

Heart disease

Research has repeatedly proven that regular exercise helps to prevent and improve heart disease. The only risk factors are doing too much too soon, placing a strain on your heart and circulatory system that it isn't ready for, or displacing an atheroma (clot or plaque), which may travel to a smaller artery and cause a blockage. Hence, it is essential that you check with your doctor before beginning running.

Once you have the go-ahead to exercise, a walking programme similar to the one outlined above may be an appropriate starting point. Depending upon your current fitness level, you may begin with either pre-run programme 1 or 2.

Insight

It's a good idea to know your blood pressure, resting pulse and cholesterol measurements before you begin, as these are all likely to improve as you increase your cardiovascular fitness, and you will find it motivating to see your health improve as well as your fitness levels.

MONITORING YOUR HEART RATE

You may want to invest in a heart rate monitor. As well as measuring your fitness parameters such as recovery rate, resting pulse, and average and maximum heart rate during exercise, it will also help you to exercise in a safe and effective heart rate training zone and may give you some peace of mind as you can monitor your cardiac activity. More information on what to look for in a heart rate monitor is included in Chapter 2 'Getting kitted out'.

If you have elevated blood pressure or high cholesterol levels, you should still check your exercise plans with your doctor before you begin, but regular running or run/walk sessions are likely to reduce your blood pressure and cholesterol levels with no detrimental effects upon your health.

Diabetes

Diabetes is linked with obesity, metabolic syndrome and heart disease, and all of these conditions benefit from reduced body weight, increased cardiovascular fitness and improved blood sugar control. If you have the go-ahead from your doctor to begin a running programme, your main consideration is managing your blood sugar levels to accommodate your running.

The main things to remember are:

▶ *Ensure you have enough energy for your run.*
▶ *A fast, high-intensity run or a long run will use up more energy.*
▶ *Make sure you refuel soon after your run.*
▶ *Allow sufficient time between runs for your carbohydrate stores to be replenished.*

FOODS FACTS

Carbohydrate-rich foods to keep you going through your run include:

▶ *porridge or meals containing oats*
▶ *rice-based meals*
▶ *pasta-based meals.*

These foods all release carbohydrate into your body quite slowly, so aim to eat them two to three hours before your run.

Quick-release carbohydrate-rich foods for fast energy include:

▶ *watermelon or watermelon juice*
▶ *banana*
▶ *white bread or white baguette*
▶ *breakfast cereals such as cornflakes*
▶ *sports drinks.*

These foods all provide energy quite quickly, so if your blood sugar is low and you need energy for a run, top up glucose levels with higher-GI (glycaemic index) foods. However, if your blood sugar control is poor and you need to avoid quick-release carbohydrates, you should manage your diet so that low- and medium-GI foods provide the energy for your runs. More information on the glycaemic index can be found in Chapter 6 'Food and drink on the run'. Sports drinks can also be useful for topping up energy mid-run if necessary – it may be a good idea to take a quickly absorbed (isotonic) sports drink or gel with you on your runs in case you run out of energy.

Insight

For a convenient and fast glucose fix, try these:

▶ *isotonic sports drink*
▶ *sports energy gel*
▶ *a handful of raisins*
▶ *a piece of chocolate.*

RUNNING IN THE EARLY DAYS

If you are not used to regular exercise, discuss your glucose and/or insulin requirements with your doctor before you begin running, as they may want to adjust your medication to accommodate your additional carbohydrate needs. It may take a while to get used to how much extra carbohydrate you need to eat to accommodate your running without overloading with glucose, so in the early days keep runs short and sweet:

▶ *Keep runs to a maximum of 20 minutes.*
▶ *Avoid higher-intensity runs such as hills or sprints.*
▶ *Plan a route close to home in case you need an energy top-up.*
▶ *Consider carrying medication or an energy gel with you.*

Osteoarthritis

Running does not cause osteoarthritis – only overuse symptoms or injuries from running increase the risk of this so-called 'wear and tear' disease. If you enjoy years of injury-free running, or react quickly and effectively to injuries and allow ample recovery time, you should not suffer osteoarthritis any more than a non-runner. However, although running can help to prevent degenerative joint and bone disease, it isn't the most ideal activity for those with an existing condition.

Insight

If done properly, running strengthens bones and joints, and reduces the occurrence of both osteoarthritis and osteoporosis. Doctors have stated that running can offset the onset of degenerative arthritis for up to 12 years – the most benefit has been found in those running between 6 and 20 miles a week.

RUNNING CONSIDERATIONS

Running may still benefit you – and your joints – if done in moderation and with the following considerations taken into account. Each person's arthritis and joint condition is individual, so check with your doctor first and don't continue with any type of exercise that causes pain or discomfort.

If you do have osteoarthritis, adhere to the following three key points:

1 *Run on softer surfaces such as grass or dirt tracks.*
2 *Combine running with intervals of power-walking.*

3 *Make sure your running shoes provide plenty of cushioning to absorb the impact from running.*

....

Insight

Consider taking a supplement such as glucosamine or chondroitin – these nutrients provide the raw materials needed to repair and renew joint cartilage, and many arthritis sufferers experience benefits from taking them.

....

Osteoporosis

Osteoporosis is reduced bone density, where the bones are more porous and more likely to fracture upon impact or with a fall. Far from causing osteoporosis, weight-bearing exercises such as running actually increase bone density and help to prevent, or at least slow down, the development of this disease.

Although osteoporosis is often found in elite female runners, the cause is actually low body weight and lack of menstruation, which in turn reduces oestrogen levels and affects the lay down of bone tissue. It is over-training and a poor diet that cause the disease, in conjunction with a very low body weight that affects hormone levels. Running may only be detrimental when osteoporosis has already been caused due to the continued impact or a fall causing a fracture.

Bone density is known to reduce after the menopause due to hormonal changes reducing the amount of bone tissue laid down – women can lose up to 20 per cent of their bone mass within just a few years of finishing the menopause, so regular running is a very positive thing to do for females.

If you can tick any number of the following boxes, you are increasing your risk of osteoporosis, and taking up or continuing running will help to offset any reduction in bone density due to these common lifestyle habits.

Factors that increase the risk of osteoporosis

Lack of regular weight-bearing exercise such as running
or walking ☐
Poor calcium or vitamin D intake ☐
High protein diet ☐
Very low body weight ☐
Missed periods or menopause ☐
Smoking ☐
Regularly consuming coffee or other caffeinated drinks ☐
Regularly consuming alcohol ☐
Advanced age ☐
Family history of osteoporosis ☐
Long-term use of steroids ☐

RUNNING CONSIDERATIONS

▶ *Running will boost your bone density, but you should choose
even ground to reduce the risk of a fall.*
▶ *Regular running will improve joint stability and muscle
strength, decreasing the risk of a fall in everyday life.*
▶ *The impact of running will increase bone density in the bones
in the lower half of your body, but you should also do weight
training to enhance the bone density of your upper body.*

Insight
You can maximize your bone density by regularly running
before and into your 30s, as this is when most bone tissue
is laid down, with bone density peaking around age 30.
However, running after age 30 will still promote optimal
bone density – if you don't use it, you lose it!

THINGS TO REMEMBER

It seems that running will benefit most health conditions and even help to prevent the occurrence of some of them. Just remember these guidelines if you are unsure of your health:

▶ *Get a pre-run check-up with your doctor before you begin.*

▶ *Get help and advice from a health and fitness coach or personal trainer.*

▶ *Take it easy to begin with.*

▶ *Listen to your body!*

… and, for injury prevention, remember these top ten tips:

▶ *Warm up thoroughly.*

▶ *Invest in good running shoes.*

▶ *Check your running posture and alignment.*

▶ *Check your running gait with the footprint test in Chapter 4.*

▶ *Don't try to progress too quickly.*

▶ *Have a menu of different runs to reduce the risk of repetitive injuries.*

▶ *Have rest days.*

▶ *Feed your body what it needs to stay in good physical condition.*

▶ *Do not run through existing injuries.*

▶ *Don't go back to running too soon after injuries or breaks.*

9

Training for an event

In this chapter you will learn:
- **what to expect on race day**
- **how to train for any running event up to and including a half marathon**
- **how to 'carb load'**.

Running events and races aren't only for competitive runners – there are dozens of charity events which have embraced the phrase 'fun running'. Although you may come first or achieve a personal best, these events are all about taking part, enjoying the run and just completing the distance.

Here are some reasons why people enter a running event:

- ✓ *for the enjoyable and social aspect of a running event*
- ✓ *for the extra motivation it provides*
- ✓ *to raise money for a charity or good cause*
- ✓ *to provide a short- or long-term running goal*
- ✓ *to compete against others.*

For many, running is all about training for the next event, but is not necessarily competitive. Each running event creates the next short-term goal, maintaining motivation and feeding the running habit. If you feel that you are lacking motivation and need an 'end goal' for your running, entering an event or race could suit you.

However, for those with a competitive edge, entering events or running races is what it's all about, and each event provides the next goal and offers running competition. There are hundreds of running events that take place throughout the year, all over the country. Whatever your level of running is, and whatever running personality you have, there is a running event to suit you!

Choosing a running event

▶ *The internet is one of the quickest and easiest ways to find out about local runs – simply do a search for runs or races in your local area, or visit some of the websites listed in the 'Taking it further' section at the end of the book. Runner's World lists all running events in the UK. Visit http://www.runnersworld.co.uk and select the events section.*

▶ *Buying a running magazine or guide is also useful for finding information about running events.*

▶ *Your local running club or health club is likely to know about local races and events.*

What to do next

1 *Check if there are any entry requirements for the run you are interested in, and if you are a beginner or novice to races, check the level of run with the organizers – you want to enter an event that you feel comfortable in and will have time to finish.*

2 *Ask about the route (or check it out if it's local) – you may be familiar with running a specific distance but there is a big difference between a flat route and an uphill run!*

3 *Check the date of the event and make sure you have enough time to train for it if you are not already running a similar distance.*

Insight
Check with run event organizers what the average (or fastest and slowest) finishing time is for the race. This will give you a good idea of the pace of the other competitors and help you to decide whether you are suited to this event, and what your running training should be geared towards.

READY TO RACE?

For a fun run of up to ten kilometres, most newcomers to running can enter as you can comfortably jog or walk/run the distance (just over six miles). There is a difference between a running event and a running race – many events are organized either for charity or to get people interested in running, and it's all about enjoying the day and completing the distance, no matter whether you run all the way or what time you complete it in.

Races, at least for some, are different, as most runners are there to win, to finish in a reasonable place or to at least run a personal best. The starting line at some of these events may be organized according to previous finishing times, so if you haven't raced before, don't expect to be at the front expecting a quick start. The good news is that you can run at your own pace, and most races, even those such as the Great North Run, will include 'fun runners' and a good amount of recovery walking!

As a guideline, here is a table of approximate run times at different levels, where runners at level 1 are likely to be competitive runners and those at level 4 are new to running, doing less running or simply running at a slower pace. Remember to build up distance or time spent running before concentrating on increasing your pace: speed becomes more important if you want to beat a personal best, increase fitness levels, or aim to compete in a timed race.

Distance	Level 1 (mins: secs OR hrs: mins)	Level 2 (mins: secs OR hrs: mins)	Level 3 (mins: secs OR hrs: mins)	Level 4 (mins: secs OR hrs: mins)
5 km (3.1 miles)	12:19–18:28	18:28–24:37	24:37–30:46	30:46–36:56
10 km (6.2 miles)	26:00–39;00	39:00–51:00	51:00–1:04	1:04–1:17
10 miles	43:00–1:04	1:04–1:25	1:25–1:46	1:46–2:08
Half marathon	57:00–1:25	1:25–1:53	1:53–2:22	2:22–2:50
Marathon	2–3 hrs	3–4 hrs	4–5 hrs	5–6 hrs

Source: www.powerrunning.com

When considering entering a race it is important to think about:

▶ *the level of the race*
▶ *the number of entrants*
▶ *the race time*
▶ *the entry fee.*

There are many running events to choose from… have a look at some of the options below, or simply log on to www.runnersworld.co.uk.

Take your pick from runs in the UK

Great Winter Run (Edinburgh, 3 miles); various Race for Life 5-km runs; 10-km BUPA runs – Great Edinburgh Run, Great Manchester Run, Great Women's Run (Sunderland), Great Wales Run (Cardiff), Great Capital Run (Hyde Park, London), Great Ireland Run (Dublin), Great Yorkshire Run (Sheffield); various Cancer Research UK 10-km runs; Great South Run (Portsmouth, 10 miles); Great North Run (Newcastle, 13.1 miles)…

If you want a good run time over shorter race distances (1–3 miles) the running training is really simple... just keep running the race distance and improving your time. As with any race, training is all about specificity – by repeating the same run that you will be doing on race day, you prepare your body (and mind) to complete the race as easily and quickly as possible. For example, the one-mile 'Killer Mile' in Mow Cop, Staffordshire, is a 25 per cent incline – something quite different to a one-mile sprint on the flat!

Insight

Remember to check out the route and terrain of your run... if it's a one-mile run up a steep hill, then most of your training runs should also be uphill; if the run is cross-country, do your training runs on the same terrain. Even better, if you live close to the race route, make this your training run for the best result.

Running programmes for a 5-km run

SIX-WEEK TRAINING PROGRAMME STARTING FROM SCRATCH

A five-kilometre run is a good goal to have if you're just starting to run, and six weeks is a good time period to train for it. If you haven't run before (or haven't run for a long time), your training programme should aim to improve your overall fitness levels but limit some runs to your five kilometre goal. You may need to begin with some recovery walking as shown – if you don't need to walk during a run, just keeping jogging, and pick up the training programme from the point that you are currently at, or advance to the next one.

	MON	TUES	WED	THURS	FRI	SAT	SUN
WEEK 1	Run 1 min Walk 2 mins: 6 times	Rest day	Run 1 min Walk 2 mins: 6 times	Rest day	Run 1 min Walk 2 mins: 6 times	Rest day	Rest day
TIME	18 mins		18 mins		18 mins		
WEEK 2	Run 2 mins Walk 2 mins: 5 times	Rest day	Run 2 mins Walk 2 mins: 5 times	Rest day	Run 2 mins Walk 2 mins: 5 times	Rest day	Rest day
TIME	20 mins		20 mins		20 mins		
WEEK 3	Run 2 mins Walk 1 min: 6 times	Rest day	Run 3 mins Walk 1 min: 5 times	Rest day	Run 3 mins Walk 1 min: 5 times	Rest day	Rest day
TIME	18 mins		20 mins		20 mins		
WEEK 4	Run 4 mins Walk 1 min: 4 times	Rest day	Run 5 mins Walk 1 min: 3 times	Rest day	Do a timed 5-km run! (or run/ walk)	Rest day	Rest day
TIME	20 mins		18 mins				
WEEK 5	Run 6 mins Walk 1 min: 3 times	Rest day	Run 6 mins Walk 1 min: 3 times	Rest day	Run 7 mins Walk 1 min: 3 times	Rest day	Rest day
TIME	21 min		21 min		24 mins		

	MON	TUES	WED	THURS	FRI	SAT	SUN
WEEK 6	Run 8 mins Walk 1 min: 2 times	Rest day	Run 9 mins Walk 1 min: 2 times	Rest day	Do a timed 5-km run!	Rest day	Race day!
TIME	18 mins		20 mins				

REMEMBER! Warm up before each run – these times do not include a warm-up.

If you have longer than six weeks to train, continue to reduce your recovery walking until you are jogging continuously for 20 minutes or more, then alternate 25-minute runs with timed five-kilometre runs until race day, making sure that the day before your event is a rest day.

SIX-WEEK TRAINING PROGRAMME FOR EXISTING RUNNERS

If you can run continuously for 20 minutes or more, you should be able to complete a five-kilometre run without recovery walking. This training programme illustrates how to make your running specific to an upcoming five-kilometre event, concentrating on:

▶ *improving overall fitness levels*
▶ *increasing your pace*
▶ *improving your 5-km time!*

This schedule combines your 'normal' runs (runs you would usually do) with timed or progressive runs to improve your running fitness.

	MON	TUES	WED	THURS	FRI	SAT	SUN
WEEK 1	Do a normal training run	Rest day	Do a timed 5-km run	Rest day	Do a normal training run	Rest day	Interval training: 5-min jog 1-min hard run
TIME	20+ mins				20+ mins		24 mins
WEEK 2	Rest day	Do a normal training run	Rest day	Interval training: 5-min jog 2-min hard run	Rest day	Do a normal training run	Rest day
TIME		20+ mins		21 mins		20+ mins	
WEEK 3	Do a timed 5-km run	Rest day	Do a normal training run, but add an extra mile	Rest day	Interval training: 4-min jog, 2-min hard run	Rest day	Do a normal training run
TIME			25+ mins		24 mins		
WEEK 4	Rest day	Interval training: 3-min jog 2-min hard run	Rest day	Do your longer training run with the extra mile	Rest day	Do a timed 5-km run	Rest day
TIME		25 mins		25+ mins			

	MON	TUES	WED	THURS	FRI	SAT	SUN
WEEK 5	Do a normal training run	Rest day	Interval training: 3-min jog 2-min hard run	Rest day	Run for 30 mins	Rest day	Do a timed 5-km run
TIME	25+ mins		30 mins		30+ mins		
WEEK 6	Rest day	Interval training: 3-min jog 2-min hard run	Rest day	Do a timed 5-km run	Rest day	Rest day	Race day!
TIME		30 mins					

If your race isn't for another week or so, just continue with a combination of longer runs, interval training and timed five-kilometre runs until race day, ensuring that you have at least one rest day before race day.

Top tips

▶ *Interval training will help you increase your five-kilometre pace, enabling you to run faster for longer stretches of your run. If you are finding the pace tough you can employ interval running techniques in your race as well – just reduce your pace over short distances if you can't maintain the speed for the entire distance.*

▶ *Try to run on similar terrain to that of the five-kilometre race, matching hills and terrain to mimic the actual run course. If you can, train on the route itself.*

▶ *If you are planning to incorporate any sprints in the race you need to include sprints in your training schedule.*

(Contd)

> ▶ *Make sure you are well warmed up before sprinting or fast-paced runs; muscles, tendons and ligaments are put under more stress during a sprint and injuries are more likely. Doing a timed five-kilometre run at the end of a longer run is good to do as you are already well warmed up.*
>
> ▶ *As you will be running your race from 'cold' (warmed up but not at the end of a run), then you should also train for this by doing stand-alone three-mile runs after a warm-up.*
>
> ▶ *Remember that high-intensity running uses up more stored carbohydrate than a slower running pace, so ensure you replace glycogen stores with complex carbohydrates in your next meal after training or racing.*

NUTRITION BEFORE, DURING AND AFTER

The higher the intensity of exercise, the more calories and the greater the proportion of carbohydrate used, so fill up on the following carbohydrate-rich meals to fuel sprint training, interval training and fast five-kilometre runs.

Carb-rich meals	
Breakfast	Porridge with chopped banana and raisins or Toasted cinnamon and raisin bagel with cream cheese
Lunch	Lentil soup with crusty bread or Baked potato with baked beans, tuna and coleslaw
Dinner	Wild rice and chicken or vegetable risotto or Spaghetti Bolognese with garlic bread
Snacks	Oat bars, nut and seed bars and yoghurt with added fruit.

We use predominantly carbohydrate during runs of 20–30 minutes. Therefore, the most important adjustment to your diet, if you have just begun to run this much regularly, is to ensure that you are eating enough carbohydrate for your increased energy requirements.

This is a short run, so there are no specific nutrition or hydration strategies required during or immediately afterwards (although you should always replenish water and carbohydrates after running).

Make sure you keep fluid levels and glycogen (carbohydrate) stores topped up throughout training, and time your pre-race meal to give you plenty of energy. See Chapter 6 'Food and drink on the run' for more information on sports nutrition.

Insight

If you are watching your weight and starting running in order to lose weight, make sure you don't consume more extra calories than you are using up, or your weight loss will stall. Stick to three meals a day, and include snacks or increase your carbohydrate intake only if you are hungry or lacking in energy. If you continue to lose weight but still have plenty of energy for your runs, you have successfully created an energy deficit. Consulting a qualified nutritionist or sports nutritionist can be helpful if you are unsure about your nutritional needs.

HYDRATION STRATEGY

You should not require additional fluid during training runs or races of this length, but you should adjust your daily fluid intake accordingly. You can calculate your individual fluid requirements as follows:

Calculating normal fluid requirements

Multiply your body weight in kilograms by 35 ml. (Convert pounds into kilograms by dividing your weight in pounds by 2.2 – there are 14 pounds in a stone.)

For example, 60 kg × 35 ml = 2,100 ml needed.

You can convert this into litres by moving the decimal point back three spaces, which gives 2.1 litres.

However, this is the amount of fluid required without considering any exercise. Drink an extra 500 ml after each run under one hour long.

Calculating how much water you need to replace after each run

You can calculate how much extra fluid you need by weighing yourself naked before and after a run (towel yourself off after your run first). Drink one litre for each kilogram (2.2 lb) of weight lost.

Running programme for a 10-km run

If you've just signed up to do a ten-kilometre run and are wondering where to start, don't worry – it's feasible to be comfortably completing ten kilometres with a six-week training schedule, though if you are starting from scratch and are not currently fit, completion rather than winning should be your goal!

This training programme focuses on improving overall fitness and endurance levels with some timed ten-kilometre runs towards the end of the six weeks. As with any of the training programmes, adapt the running programme to suit you and to fit into the training period you have before your race or running event:

▶ *Start at the level or week that suits you.*
▶ *Stick at a week if you're struggling or have had to miss one or two runs.*
▶ *Feel free to fit in an extra run at the weekend if you feel good, but always try to have a rest day between runs.*
▶ *Although you should reduce the recovery walking as quickly as you can, early weeks of running should be more about putting the time and distance in rather than trying to speed up your pace. If this is your first ten-kilometre run, you should be aiming to complete it, rather than run an under-50 minutes time!*

SIX-WEEK TRAINING PROGRAMME STARTING FROM SCRATCH (10 KM)

	MON	TUES	WED	THURS	FRI	SAT	SUN
WEEK 1	Run 1 min Walk 2 mins: 6 times	Rest day	Run 1 min Walk 2 mins: 2 times	Rest day	Run 1 min Walk 2 mins: 6 times	Rest day	Rest day
TIME	18 mins		18 mins		18 mins		

	MON	TUES	WED	THURS	FRI	SAT	SUN
WEEK 2	Run 2 mins Walk 2 mins: 5 times	Rest day	Run 2 mins Walk 2 mins: 5 times	Rest day	Run 2 mins Walk 2 mins: 6 times	Rest day	Rest day
TIME	20 mins		20 mins		24 mins		
WEEK 3	Run 2 mins Walk 1 min: 7 times	Rest day	Run 3 mins Walk 1 min: 6 times	Rest day	Run 3 mins Walk 1 min: 7 times	Rest day	Rest day
TIME	24 mins		28 mins		20 mins		
WEEK 4	Run 4 mins Walk 1 min: 5 times	Rest day	Run 5 mins Walk 1 min: 4 times	Rest day	Run 5 mins Walk 1 min: 6 times	Rest day	Rest day
TIME	25 mins		24 mins		36 mins		
WEEK 5	Run 6 mins Walk 1 min: 5 times	Rest day	Run 8 mins Walk 1 min: 4 times	Rest day	Do a timed 10 km! Expect to take about 1 hr	Rest day	Rest day
TIME	35 mins		36 mins		1 hour		
WEEK 6	Run 10 mins Walk 1 min: 4 times	Rest day	Run 12 mins Walk 1 min: 3 times	Rest day	Do an easy jog for 40 mins	Rest day	Rest day
TIME	44 mins		39 mins				

As you can see, building up to run continuously for approximately an hour or to run ten kilometres is tough to do within six weeks unless you have a good fitness base to begin with. If you have a little longer to train, continue with runs of 40 minutes at a moderate pace combined with timed ten-kilometre runs until race day.

SIX-WEEK TRAINING PROGRAMME FOR EXISTING RUNNERS (10 KM)

If you can run continuously for 20 minutes or more and have six weeks or longer to train for your ten-kilometre run, you may be able to complete it in under an hour. This training programme concentrates on three things:

1 *Improving overall fitness levels.*
2 *Increasing your pace.*
3 *Improving your 10-km time.*

	MON	TUES	WED	THURS	FRI	SAT	SUN
WEEK 1	Do a normal training run	Rest day	Interval training: 5-min jog, 2-min hard run	Rest day	Add 1 mile to your training run	Rest day	Run for 40 mins
TIME	20+ mins		28 mins		30+ mins		40 mins
WEEK 2	Rest day	Interval training: 5 min-jog 2-min hard run	Rest day	Run for 40 mins	Rest day	Do a timed 10-km run	Rest day
TIME		35 mins		40 mins			

	MON	TUES	WED	THURS	FRI	SAT	SUN
WEEK 3	Interval training: 5-min jog 2-min hard run	Rest day	Run for 45 mins	Rest day	Interval training: 4-min jog 2-min hard run	Rest day	Do a timed 10-km run
TIME	42 mins		45 mins		42 mins		
WEEK 4	Rest day	Easy jog 30–40 mins	Rest day	Interval training: 4-min jog, 2-min hard run	Rest day	Run for 45 mins	Rest day
TIME				48 mins		45 mins	
WEEK 5	Do a normal 45–50 min run	Rest day	Do a timed 10-km run	Rest day	Interval training 4-min jog, 2-min hard run	Rest day	Do a 50-min run
TIME	40–50 mins				54 mins		50 mins
WEEK 6	Rest day	Interval training: 4-min jog, 2-min hard run	Rest day	Do a timed 10-km run	Rest day	Rest day	Race day!
TIME		54 mins					

If your race isn't for another week or so, just continue with a combination of long runs, interval training and timed ten-kilometre runs until race day, ensuring that you have at least one rest day before race day.

NUTRITION BEFORE, DURING AND AFTER

Running for 40 minutes or longer three to four times a week is a good running habit that needs fuelling. Make sure you eat three meals a day with snacks in between if you need the extra energy. Combine complex carbohydrates for energy with protein foods to maintain strong muscles and joints, enhance recovery and reduce the risk of injury.

Rehydrating during a ten-kilometre race or training run should not be necessary as long as you are well hydrated beforehand. Follow this sample nutrition menu to enhance fluid and carbohydrate stores, and rehydrate afterwards by drinking about one litre of water or hypotonic sports drink.

Seven-day eating plan for 10-km training

This is a simple eating plan that avoids the need to weigh foods –
you only need to monitor your water intake.

- ✓ *Each meal is based upon starchy carbohydrates with a low to medium GI.*
- ✓ *The meals are well balanced with ample protein, fats, fibre and nutrients.*
- ✓ *Snacks are carbohydrate-rich.*
- ✓ *If you need to increase your carbohydrate intake, simply add an extra carb-rich snack during the afternoon or for supper.*
- ✓ *Although the foods in this eating plan also contain water, you should calculate your individual fluid requirements for your body weight and ensure that you drink this throughout the day, drinking 500 ml to one litre of water extra for each run that you do (more for longer runs).*
- ✓ *Move snacks and meals around to accommodate your runs – main meals should be eaten at least two hours before running, snacks one hour before.*

Monday

Breakfast	Porridge made with milk, added mixed seeds and a banana
Snack	Mixed-fruit salad with yoghurt and mixed nuts
Lunch	Baked potato with tuna, beans and a mixed salad
Snack	Wholewheat scone or muffin with butter and jam
Dinner	Baked salmon steak with broccoli, cauliflower and baked sweet potato

Tuesday

Breakfast	Muesli with milk, chopped banana, berries and mixed nuts
Snack	Nut/seed bar and a mixed-berry smoothie
Lunch	Mixed-bean salad with chickpeas and brown rice, tomatoes, garlic, onions, cucumber, radish, celery and tomatoes
Dinner	Pasta with chicken and vegetables

Wednesday

Breakfast	Two toasted bagels with cream cheese and two scrambled eggs
Snack	Oat-based sugar-free cereal bar and fresh fruit
Lunch	Tuna or ham salad sandwich with juice and a cereal bar
Snack	Nut/seed or cereal bar and a piece of fruit
Dinner	Brown rice with roasted root vegetables, tuna steak and broccoli

Thursday

Breakfast	Porridge or millet with added yoghurt, mixed nuts and fruit
Snack	Banana and berry smoothie
Lunch	Tortilla wraps with avocado, salad, mozzarella and pine nuts
Snack	Mixed-fruit salad with yoghurt and mixed nuts
Dinner	Mixed stuffed peppers and stuffed potatoes with vegetables

Friday

Breakfast	Granola with added yoghurt and fruit
Snack	Cereal bar and glass of juice or milk
Lunch	Thick vegetable and barley soup served with crusty bread
Snack	Nut/seed bar and a mixed-berry smoothie
Dinner	Bean and vegetable curry or chilli with steamed brown rice

Saturday

Breakfast	Porridge or granola with added yoghurt and fruit
Snack	Wholewheat scone or muffin with butter and jam
Lunch	Lentil soup with soda bread
Snack	Banana and berry smoothie
Dinner	Steamed fish with garlic-roasted carrots, potatoes and broccoli

Breakfast	Two poached eggs with baked beans on wholewheat toast
Snack	Nut/seed or cereal bar and a piece of fruit
Lunch	Roast Sunday dinner
Snack	Yoghurt and mixed nuts
Dinner	Tuna salad sandwich

Insight

▶ *Add an extra supper snack if you need additional energy or carbohydrates.*

▶ *Don't forget to drink enough water in addition to this eating plan.*

▶ *Eating smaller meals throughout the day will help you to store more carbohydrate as glycogen and make better use of the protein eaten, rather than storing excess as fat if too much is consumed in one meal.*

If you need more or less carbohydrate, you can add or subtract carbohydrate foods from the eating plan in 50 g portion sizes until you find the right intake for your activity level.

For example

Here are a few ideas of what 50 g and 100 g of carbohydrate look like:

Snacks providing approximately 50 g of carbohydrate:
Bowl of cereal with milk and added fruit
Medium-sized jacket potato with salad and a filling
A filled sandwich with two slices of bread.

Meals providing approximately 100 g of carbohydrate:
120 g of pasta (pre-cooked weight) with sauce and vegetables
Risotto containing 120 g of rice (pre-cooked weight)
Bean casserole containing 200 g of beans/lentils (dry weight).

Running programme for a half marathon

If you are new to running, then a half marathon is not likely to be your first running event. If, however, you are a novice runner but would like to complete a half marathon (or even a marathon), simply work through the running programmes throughout this book to build up your distance and pace until you can comfortably complete a ten-kilometre run – from this point you are ready to begin training for a half marathon.

Although once you can run for an hour or run ten kilometres, you are likely to be able to complete a half marathon (just over twice a 10-km run), you will still benefit from training to run the distance of a half marathon. Although lots of people enter half marathons and do complete the distance, it's good to feel comfortable and enjoy the run – and a good run time is always an added bonus!

This training programme takes the average ten-kilometre runner up to half-marathon status over 12 weeks, concentrating on increasing running distance whilst maintaining pace.

12-WEEK SAMPLE TRAINING PROGRAMME FOR A HALF MARATHON

	MON	TUES	WED	THURS	FRI	SAT	SUN
WEEK 1	Do a normal training run	Rest day	Interval training: 3-min jog, 2-min hard run	Rest day	Run a timed 10 km	Rest day	Run for 7 miles
TIME	40+ mins		40 mins				

	MON	TUES	WED	THURS	FRI	SAT	SUN
WEEK 2	Rest day	Interval training: 5-min jog 2-min hard run	Rest day	Hit the hills for a 30-min run	Rest day	Rest day	Run for 8 miles
TIME		42 mins		30 mins			
WEEK 3	Rest day	Rest day	Interval training: 3-min jog, 2-min hard run	Rest day	Run a timed 10 km	Rest day	Run for 8 miles
TIME			50 mins				
WEEK 4	Rest day	Hit the hills for a 30-min run	Rest day	Interval training: 3-min jog, 2-min hard run	Rest day	Do a timed 9-mile run	Rest day
TIME		30 mins		50 mins			
WEEK 5	Rest day	Do a 10-km run	Rest day	Interval training: 3-min jog 2-min hard run	Rest day	Do a timed 9-mile run	Rest day
TIME				55 mins			

(Contd)

	MON	TUES	WED	THURS	FRI	SAT	SUN
WEEK 6	Rest day	Do a steady 1-hour run	Rest day	Interval training: 3-min jog 2-min hard run	Rest day	Rest day	Hit the hills for a 40-min run
TIME		1 hour		55 mins			40 mins
WEEK 7	Rest day	Do a 10-km run	Rest day	Rest day	Run for 10 miles	Rest day	Rest day
TIME							
WEEK 8	Do a steady, 1 hour run	Rest day	Interval training: 1-min jog, 2-min hard run	Rest day	Rest day	Run for 11 miles	Rest day
TIME	60 mins		60 mins				
WEEK 9	Rest day	Do a timed 12-mile run	Rest day	Rest day	Hit the hills for a 40-min run	Rest day	Do a timed 10-km run
TIME					40 mins		
WEEK 10	Rest day	Do a timed 12-mile run	Rest day	Rest day	Interval training: 1-min jog 2-min hard run	Rest day	Rest day
TIME					60 mins		

	MON	TUES	WED	THURS	FRI	SAT	SUN
WEEK 11	Hit the hills for a 40-min run	Rest day	Rest day	Do a timed 12-mile run (or 13.1 if you want to)	Rest day	Rest day	Do a 10-km run
TIME	40 mins						
WEEK 12	Rest day	Interval training: 1-min jog 2-min hard run	Rest day	Easy run for 30 mins	Rest day	Rest day	Race day!
TIME		60 mins					

If you have more time before your half marathon, simply continue combining long runs just under the half-marathon distance with some interval training and ten-kilometre runs. You can run the full distance if you want to, but, if you can run 12 miles, you'll definitely be able to complete the 13.1 miles on race day!

Insight

Successful running results are due to a combination of:

1 *your running*
2 *good nutrition*
3 *sufficient rest.*

Make sure you allow enough rest days in your training schedule to replenish energy levels and allow muscles and joints to recover. This is especially important after longer runs and in the week prior to your half marathon.

NUTRITION

During training

Nutrition becomes more important as you run more often and for longer distances. Each element of a healthy diet is essential to your success – Chapter 6 'Food and drink on the run' provides more detailed information on sports nutrition, but here's a quick overview.

Nutrient	Why endurance runners need it	How much you need
Carbohydrate	For energy on all runs	8–10 g per kg body weight
Protein	For recovery and strength	1.2–1.4 g per kg body weight
Fat	For energy on longer runs	25 per cent of total energy intake (approx. 55 g per day based upon a daily food intake of 2,000 kcal)
Water	For optimum hydration	35 ml per kg body weight plus 500 ml after short runs and one litre after runs of one hour plus

As you run more, you can – and will – eat more. The extra calories should come from an increase of all nutrients, but the proportion of carbohydrate should also increase a little to provide the extra energy. If you have lost weight since you began running, you will require less food as your body weight has reduced. However, you could also adjust your diet by ensuring 60 per cent of your total food intake consists of carbohydrates at the ten-kilometre run level, and may increase this a little more if you are running at half-marathon level.

In short, the more you run the more carbohydrate you need to eat.

During the race

Your carbohydrate and fluid requirements during a half marathon will depend largely on your pre-race nutrition. If you have maximized fluid and carbohydrate levels prior to beginning your race, you are much less likely to become dehydrated, and will require less fluid and energy during your run. Bearing in mind that it is easier to eat and drink before you run rather than during your run, this is essential for a comfortable and successful race.

Insight
You are unlikely to be able to make up for starting a long run already dehydrated or lacking in energy during, so good pre-run nutrition is essential for success.

However, if you are running for 90 minutes or more, it is likely that you will need to rehydrate and refuel. A combination of plain water and isotonic sports drinks consumed in small amounts throughout the half marathon should provide the fluid and energy top-ups you require.

After the race
Remember these three key points:

1 *Continue to replace fluid with water and sports drinks.*
2 *Continue to replenish energy stores with carbohydrate-rich foods within the first 40 minutes if possible, or certainly within the first two hours after finishing.*
3 *Continue to take in fluids and carbohydrates at least every two hours for the next 48 hours.*

HYDRATION STRATEGY

Your water intake should increase to match the quantity of running you are doing, and, as carbohydrate or calorie intake increases, your fluid intake should increase as well. You should allow approximately 750 ml of water for each hour of running – more in warm weather.

As your intake of carbohydrates and water are the two most important elements of your diet during endurance running, watch out for these tell-tale signs to adjust your diet:

▶ *Your urine should be plentiful and a pale straw colour – if it is any darker you need to drink more water.*
▶ *If you feel thirsty, you need to increase your water intake.*

> ▶ *If you lack energy during your run, you may need to drink more.*
> ▶ *If you lack energy, feel tired or are failing to increase your running distance or pace, you may need more carbohydrates in your diet (or you may need more recovery time).*

Running for over an hour

If you are running for over an hour whilst training, you may need to consume fluid during the run. It is essential to ensure full hydration prior to a run of this length, but drinking options during your run are as follows:

> ▶ *You could arrange a route that goes near your house halfway through and plan a swift cup of water at that point.*
> ▶ *You could do the same at a friend's house en route.*
> ▶ *You could plan your route past a public water fountain.*
> ▶ *You could opt to carry some water with you (see the water bottle options in Chapter 2 'Getting kitted out').*
> ▶ *You could plan long runs with a cycle buddy who can carry some water for you. This also provides company, motivation and a good pace on longer runs.*

Insight

As you will want to take some water on board during your half marathon, part of your training for such an event should be practising drinking whilst running. It is important to know when you need to drink, how much you can drink to hydrate adequately without feeling uncomfortable, and what fluid suits you best – before race day.

Planning your hydration strategy for race day

Water is the main nutrient you will need during a half marathon. You may need additional carbohydrate, but this will come in the form of a sports drink anyway, so your hydration strategy is doubly important. During your longer training runs, it is essential to find out:

> ▶ *how much fluid you need to drink throughout the previous day(s) to be fully hydrated for a long run*

- *how much fluid you will need over a half-marathon distance*
- *how much fluid you can drink and continue running comfortably*
- *whether you prefer water or a hypotonic or isotonic sports drink.*

Race day is not the time to experiment with different drinks or drinking whilst running for the first time.

Carb loading pre-race

As with your hydration strategy, carbohydrate loading should be tried and tested with long training runs so that you discover what works best for you and can perfect your pre-race nutrition plan. As some of your training runs will be long runs taking between one and two hours, you may benefit from carb loading for these runs anyway.

Carbohydrate loading is frequently used to enhance performance in endurance events such as a half marathon or marathon. It involves adjusting your dietary intake and training programme to maximize the amount of energy you can store. As we normally store about one and a half hours' worth of glycogen (carbohydrate energy) in our liver and muscles, you should not need to 'carb load' unless your event or training session is likely to involve running for more than that amount of time. So, although you need enough carbohydrates in your diet for regular running, the half marathon or marathon is where this technique becomes really useful.

Insight

Remember, the higher the intensity of your running, the higher the proportion of carbohydrate in your fuel mix. So, even if you complete a half marathon in approximately 90 minutes, if you have run faster, you will have used up more carbohydrate and are still likely to have depleted your carbohydrate stores. Carbohydrate usage is affected by both run time and speed so, for a higher-intensity run you may still benefit from carb loading or use of isotonic sports drinks during the run.

CARB-LOADING REGIME

This technique originally involved a combination of glycogen-depleting, higher-intensity exercise and a reduction in carbohydrate intake followed by a high-carbohydrate diet with very little exercise for three days prior to an event. Reducing the amount of carbohydrate encourages glycogen synthetase (the enzyme that stores glycogen) to store more glycogen than normal, and the adaptations in exercise have the following effect:

▶ *High-intensity exercise depletes glycogen stores, prompting storage.*
▶ *A rest phase or low-intensity exercise keeps glycogen stores high.*

However, reducing carbohydrate intake reduces the energy available to run and will affect your training schedule. It is also possible to not consume enough carbohydrate to replace glycogen stores during the final high-carbohydrate phase of the carb-loading diet.

Current recommendations for carb-loading techniques include a high carbohydrate intake immediately prior to an event, but without the initial low carbohydrate intake. Exercise is used to deplete carbohydrate stores and promote additional glycogen storage. By continuing with a normal amount of carbohydrate in the diet, energy levels are maintained and running can continue as required, although overall training intensity in the few days prior to a race or event should be reduced in order to encourage optimal glycogen stores.

Carb loading can be done over a week or even in one day prior to an event. It is important for you to try out both programmes to see what suits you best; although a one-day schedule is easier to plan, you may find it difficult to consume large amounts of carbohydrate over such a short period of time.

Over a week

This table shows a recommended programme for carbohydrate loading during the final week prior to your half marathon. Carbohydrate has been abbreviated to CHO.

Day 1	Day 2	Day 3	Day 4	Day 5	Day 6	Day 7
Normal diet	Moderate CHO diet (5–7 g CHO per kg body weight)	Moderate CHO diet (5–7 g CHO per kg body weight)	High CHO diet (8–10 g CHO per kg body weight)	High CHO diet (8–10 g CHO per kg body weight)	High CHO diet (8–10 g CHO per kg body weight)	Race day
Endurance run of approx. 10 miles – this will be your last long run prior to your race	Rest day	Rest day	Moderate run of approx. 45 mins	Rest day	Rest day	Race day

Over just one day

This table shows how you can deplete and maximize carbohydrate stores by incorporating an intense exercise session into your schedule the day before race day.

Day 1	Day 2	Day 3	Day 4	Day 5	Day 6	Day 7
Normal diet	Normal diet	Normal diet	High CHO diet (8 g CHO per kg body weight)	High CHO diet (8 g CHO per kg body weight)	High CHO diet (10 g CHO per kg body weight]	Race day

(Contd)

Day 1	Day 2	Day 3	Day 4	Day 5	Day 6	Day 7
Endurance run of approx. 10 miles – this will be your last long run prior to your race	Rest day	Moderate run of approx. 45 mins	Rest day	Rest day	Thorough warm-up followed by 3 mins' high-intensity sprint	Race day

If you try this programme, make sure that you warm up very thoroughly for your three-minute sprint – remember that sprinting increases the risk of injury and that is the last thing you want the day before your half marathon.

Tips for carbohydrate loading on both programmes:

▶ *Eat a high-carbohydrate diet at all times.*
▶ *Eat a carbohydrate-rich meal or snack 1–4 hours prior to training or competition to maximize glycogen stores and available energy.*
▶ *Choose low- or medium-GI foods depending on the timing of your last meal.*
▶ *Begin to drink an isotonic sports drink within the first half hour to ensure that you have enough energy for your race.*
▶ *Continue to base meals and snacks on carbohydrates during the post-exercise period. It could take as long as 48 hours to replenish glycogen stores fully.*

Insight

Each gram of stored glycogen holds approximately three grams of water with it, so increasing your glycogen stores may increase your body weight by a few pounds. This is another reason to test carb loading before race day – the extra weight may be more detrimental than the extra energy is helpful!

Basic rules for *any* race!

Of course your running event may not be a three-mile (5-km) or a ten-kilometre run or a half marathon, but you should be able to adjust the training and nutrition guidelines to suit any event – trail running, fell running, cross-country, sprinting – of any distance, by remembering these six basic rules.

1   Specificity – tailor your training to match the terrain and distance of the run you aim to complete, run the exact route if you can, and even run at the same time of day if possible.

2   Give yourself enough time – plan your running progress so that you are already running at the pace, or completing the distance, before your event.

3   To decide whether you will be ready for a race or running event, work backwards from the event date, considering how much further or faster you can progress each week, and see how long it will take to get from your current running level to what is required.

4   The higher the intensity and longer duration of a running event, the more essential it is to maximize fluid and energy levels, and replenish water and carbohydrate thoroughly after each training session and after your event.

5   Always taper training immediately before your event to maximize glycogen stores and allow you to enter your event well rested.

6   Practise everything during training – this includes new kit (definitely new trainers), different hydration strategies and eating different foods. Once something is tried and tested and you know what works best for you, then you are ready for race day.

Race day

Your first running event can be a nerve-wracking experience until you actually begin running. As with anything new, not knowing what to expect, where to go and what to do can be unsettling. Preparation is essential before and on race day. Being organized will make the difference between an enjoyable day and nightmare scenarios such as forgetting your trainers or race number, not eating properly or having to drive home in wet, sweaty clothes.

It is likely that you will receive race or event information prior to the day, so have a thorough read through the literature and make a list of things you need to take with you. You may be able to register on race day, but this means you might not have vital race information such as the running route until the day of the race. If you enter within a week or two of the race, you may also have to wait to pick up your entry pack on the day, so try to register early whenever possible. Some races do have limited entry numbers, so, if you are serious about entering, do it sooner rather than later. Once you have committed to an event, this will also provide fresh momentum and motivation and a new training goal for your runs.

Insight

Some races pre-register through the post, but if you have to register on race day, leave enough time to queue, particularly for big races. However, you don't want to have too much time before racing as this is when nerves can set in. Try to plan your arrival so you have enough time to register and get ready, but won't be hanging around for too long.

BEFORE RACE DAY

Apart from making a list to help organization and avoid forgetting anything (racing around on the morning of the event is not good pre-race preparation!), there are a few other things that will help your race or event go well on the big day. There are five main areas to focus on:

1 *Training for the event (6–12 weeks before).*
2 *Proper nutrition to support good training gains (6–12 weeks before).*
3 *The location of the event and planning how you will get there, allowing plenty of time for your journey.*
4 *Pre-race nutrition and hydration strategy (48 hours prior to race or longer if a carbohydrate-loading strategy is relevant).*
5 *Preparing your race kit etc. a day or two before race day.*

Many runners, especially those new to event running, will not give a thought to what they eat and drink until race day, and will be rushing around trying to get everything organized on the morning of the event. Poor planning can easily result in arriving late or forgetting something vital, and this is highly likely to affect your focus during the event. It is essential that you time your meals and plan what to eat prior to race day to avoid problems such as running out of porridge or not having your favourite sports drink available.

Insight

If your run is important to you, then place the relevant amount of importance on preparing for it. Don't let months of training go to waste because you didn't prepare properly.

List for race day
Don't forget:

✓ *race information and number if sent*
✓ *safety pins or number belt to attach number to vest*
✓ *kit for the race (socks, running kit, underwear and/or support bra)*
✓ *running shoes*
✓ *heart rate monitor if you use one – pre-programmed for the race if necessary*
✓ *warm sweatshirt or fleece for before and after the race*

- ✓ *sweat bottoms for before or after the race*
- ✓ *spare pair of trainers or shoes for after the race in wet weather*
- ✓ *change of clothes and shower toiletries if there are facilities*
- ✓ *toilet paper*
- ✓ *painkillers in case of a last-minute headache or stomach ache*
- ✓ *water and/or sports drinks*
- ✓ *flask of coffee, if appropriate*
- ✓ *pre- and post-race snacks and meals, depending on race timing*
- ✓ *sun cream if applicable*
- ✓ *money for sports drinks, hot drinks and food and for browsing stalls*
- ✓ *camera (if you have a friend or partner to capture you running across the finish line!).*

Insight

Take some toilet paper with you on race day! The toilets may be in a building or may be portable loos; either way, on race day there is never enough toilet paper and the last thing you want is pre-run nerves prompting the runs and no toilet paper!

IMMEDIATELY BEFORE THE RACE

Make sure you are warmed up before you begin running. You certainly need to warm up for sprints and fast races, and even for a half marathon it is best to warm up first so that you can begin at a good pace. Jogging around for ten minutes will enable you to get off to a good start.

Mental preparation

If getting a good time in your race or event is important to you, you need to know what mental preparation works for you and how you are going to fit it into your pre-run ritual. It may simply be focusing on the run whilst you do your warm-up, or spending a couple of minutes alone immediately before the race begins.

If you have friends or family with you, make sure they know beforehand if you need time alone to do your warm-up or for mental preparation. It may be easier to think of the race start as ten minutes before you actually begin running, so you say goodbye and have time to focus on the run ahead without distractions.

....

Insight

Having someone with you is not only great moral support, but is also really useful on a practical basis. For instance, you can leave your sweat top on until the last minute then leave it with them, rather than have to take your belongings back to the car or a locker, which may be quite a distance from the starting point of the race.

....

The next step... running a marathon?

Many event runners stick to running five- or ten-kilometre races, and based upon research stating that once you can run continuously for 40 minutes or more, there is little need to run any further, you may not feel the need to experience a half marathon.

However, for those of you who have squeezed every ounce of advice from this book, conquered the half marathon and would like to take your running to the next level, you can always take advantage of the expert guidance in *Be Your Best at Marathon Running* (see the details in 'Taking it further').

But, whatever your running choices are – whether you pound the streets or run in the woods; whether you run around the block for 20 minutes or jog for more than an hour, and whether you run a marathon with thousands of other runners or enjoy the solitude of it being just you and the road – here's to many more happy miles!

THINGS TO REMEMBER

▶ *Find an event to suit you – revisit 'choosing a running event' at the start of this chapter for inspiration.*

▶ *Plan your training so that you know you can complete the distance and achieve your planned race time easily when you stand on the start line.*

▶ *Be organized to avoid problems on race day.*

▶ *Plan time alone before the race if you need it.*

▶ *Have a warm-up routine that helps to focus your mind on the run.*

Taking it further

Books

Bean, Anita *The Complete Guide to Sports Nutrition* (A&C Black Publishers Ltd., 2009)

Blades, Mabel *The Glycemic Load Counter: A Pocket Guide to Gl and GI Values for Over 800 Foods* (Ulysses Press, 2008)

Dreyer, Danny and Dreyer, Katherine *Chi Running: A Revolutionary Approach to Effortless, Injury-Free Running* (Fireside, 2009)

Glover, B. and Glover, S. *The Competitive Runner's Handbook* (Penguin, 1999)

Murphy, Sam *Run for Life: The Real Woman's Guide to Running* (Kyle Cathie, 2003)

Rogers, Tim *Be Your Best at Marathon Running* (Hodder Education, 2010)

Romanov, Nicholas *Dr. Nicholas Romanov's Pose Method of Running* (Pose Tech Press, 2004)

MAGAZINES

Runner's World

Running Times

Trail Runner

Online

RUNNING WEBSITES

www.roadrunnersclub.org.uk
www.runnersworld.co.uk
www.runnersworld.com
www.running4women.com
www.runningtimes.com
www.trailrunnermag.com

RUNNING ACCESSORIES

www.coolrunning.com
www.fitbug.com
www.heartratemonitor.co.uk
www.nikeplus.com
www.pedometer.com
www.pedometers.co.uk
www.polarpersonaltrainer.com
www.polarusa.com
www.runningplanet.com
www.runningwarehouse.com

ONLINE RUNNING JOURNALS

www.fitnessjournal.org
www.running-log.com

FOR HOME TREADMILLS

www.technogym.com
www.lifefitness.com

FOR BALANCE TRAINING, WOBBLE BOARDS AND FOAM ROLLERS

www.performbetter.com
www.physiosupplies.com

RUNNING METHODS

www.chirunning.com
www.posetech.com
www.powerrunning.com

TO CALCULATE YOUR PACE

www.coolrunning.com/engine/4/4_1/96.shtml

BLEEP TEST PACKAGES

www.overdrivefitness.com
www.thebleeptest.com
www.topendsports.com

BREATHING EXERCISES AND INSPIRATORY MUSCLE TRAINING

www.polarpersonaltrainer.com
www.powerbreathe.com

FOR GAIT ANALYSIS IN THE UK

www.profeet.co.uk
http://running.timeoutdoors.com

EVENT INFORMATION

www.cancerresearchuk.org/10k
www.doitforcharity.com
www.greatrun.org
www.london-marathon.co.uk
www.raceforlife.co.uk
www.rrca.org
www.runnersworld.co.uk
www.runningintheusa.com

TO LOCATE A SPORTS NUTRITIONIST OR DIETICIAN

www.bant.org.co.uk
www.clickfortherapy.com
www.nctc.ul.ie/ServicesDirectory/files/National_Register_For_
  Accredited_Sports_Nutritionists.doc (Ireland)
www.nutripeople.co.uk
www.nutrition.bitwine.com
www.pro-activate.co.uk

Index

abdominal (core) muscles, *68–9, 170*
abductors, stretching, *80–1*
active rest, *168*
adductors, stretching, *80*
alignment, *65–71, 160–6*
allergies, *213–15*
American College of Sports Medicine, *2, 113*
amino acids, *115*
ankles, injury, *199–202*
antioxidants, *139, 184*
arms, position, *68*
asthma, *212–13*

babies, running with, *219*
back
    muscles, *68–9*
    stretching, *81–2*
balance
    during pregnancy, *216–17*
    training, *201–2*
beaches, running on, *53–4*
Bean, Anita
bleep test, *150*
blood pressure, *2–3*
blood sugar and diabetes, *226*
bone density, *228–9*
bone strength, *4–5*
bottom, stretching, *78–9*
bowel problems, *180–1*
bras, *18–19*
breakfast, *121–2*
breaks, returning to running, *108–9*
breathing, *4, 73–4, 178*
    problems, *212–13*
building blocks, goals as, *105–6*

caffeine, *139–42*
calf stretches, *75–6*
calories
    expenditure, *6, 11, 220*
    and weight loss, *125*
camber, *50, 54*
carb loading, *137, 257–60*
    see also carbohydrates

carbohydrates (CHO), *37–8, 112–14, 117–21*
    post-run, *135–7*
    stores, *126*
    see also carb loading
Chi running, *164–6*
CHD (coronary heart disease), *3*
CHO, *see* carbohydrates
cholesterol, *3*
circadian rhythm, *45*
circuit training, *169*
clothing, *18–21*
company, *88–93*
cooling down, *74–83*
coronary heart disease (CHD), *3*
cramp, *175–7*
cross-country running, *52–3*
cross-training, *146, 168–71*
cycling, *168*

daytime running, *122*
dehydration, *see* hydration
delayed onset muscle soreness (DOMS), *182–4*
depression, *10*
de-training, effects, *50*
diabetes, *225–7*
diarrhoea, *180–1*
dissociation, *86–9, 100*
distance, *49*
    increasing, *155, 156*
DOMS (delayed onset muscle soreness), *182–4*
drinks, *60–1*
    energy, *128, 131–3*
Dryer, Danny, *164*
dynamic stretching, *66*

earache, *20*
endorphins, *8, 10*
energy
    foods for, *112–14, 116, 117–24*
    levels, *7*
    replenishing, *127–8*

energy drinks, *128, 131–3*
    for cramp, *177*
equipment list for races, *263–4*
ergogenic aids, *139–42*
evening running, *44, 122*
events
    5-km runs, *235–41*
    10-km runs, *242–9*
    choosing, *232–3, 234–5*
    entering, *262*
    half marathons, *250–60*
    preparation for, *262–5*
    vs. races, *233*
exercises, strengthening, *208–10*
extrinsic motivation, *94*

fartlek training, *151*
fast twitch muscles, *171–2*
fat, *112–13, 116, 117–18*
feet
    footfall, *17, 71–3*
    injury, *195–9*
    and Pose running, *162–4*
FIT(T) principle, *153–7*
fitness, specific, *32–3*
fitness classes, *169*
fluids, *60–1, 129–31*
    for events, *241*
    for half marathons, *255–7*
food, *60–1*
    for 10-km runs, *246–9*
    and diabetes, *225–6*
    during run, *127*
    for events, *240–1*
    groups, *112*
    for half marathons, *254–5*
    planning meals, *121–4*
    post-run, *136–7*
foot pods, *23*
footfall, *17, 71–3*
    see also feet
form, running, *160–6*
frequency, increasing, *154, 156*
fuel mix, *117–18*
fun runs, *233*

gait, *71–3*
gastrocnemius muscles, *75–6*
gluteal muscles
    injury, *193–4*
    stretching, *78–9*
glycaemic index (GI), *118–19, 121*

glycaemic load (GL), *120–1*
glycogen stores, *126, 136–7, 258, 260*
goals, setting, *101–7*

habits, building, *95–101*
half marathons, *250–60*
hamstrings, stretching, *76–7*
hay fever, *213–15*
head, alignment, *67–8*
headwear, *20–1*
health conditions, *212–29*
heart, *2–3*
    disease, *224–5*
heart rate (HR) training, *24–5,*
 157–60
heel spurs, *195–6*
Hernelahti, M. et al., *2–3*
high-density lipoprotein (HDL), *3*
hill running, *39, 147–8*
hips
    alignment, *69–70*
    stretching, *79–80*
'hitting the wall', *116*
hormones in pregnancy, *217*
hot weather, *134*
hydration, *21, 129–31*
    during run, *133–5*
    for events, *241*
    for half marathons, *255–7*
    post-run, *135–6*
hypertension, *2–3*
hypertonic drinks, *132*
hypotonic drinks, *131*

iliopsoas, stretching, *79–80*
iliotibial (IT) band
    injury, *190–2*
    stretching, *80–1*
injury
    ankles, *199–202*
    avoiding, *174*
    causes, *187–9*
    feet, *195–9*
    gluteus medius muscles, *193–4*
    IT band, *190–2*
    knees, *194*
    prevention, *186–7, 207–12*
    shin splints, *204–7*
    tendons, *202–4*
intensity
    increasing, *39–40, 154, 156*
    reducing, *207–8*

interval training, *39, 151–2*
intrinsic motivation, *93–4*
isotonic drinks, *131–2*
    for cramp, *177*
IT band, *see* iliotibial (IT) band

jackets, *19–20*
joints, *227–8*

kit list for races, *263–4*
knees
    alignment, *70*
    injury, *194*

lactic acid, *182*
landmarks, en route, *58–9*
legs, stretching, *75–8, 80–1*
length of route, *49*
ligament tears, ankles, *200–1*
ligaments, *5*
logging, online, *60*
low-density lipoprotein (LDL), *3*
lunchtime running, *43*

marathons, *265*
markers, en route, *58–9*
massage, *184–6*
maternity belts, *216*
Maximum Heart Rate, calculation,
  157–8
metabolism, *6*
method, *160–6*
minerals, *116–17*
    supplement, *139*
mood, enhancement, *8–9*
morning running, *42, 121–2*
motivation, *58–9, 88, 89–94, 97–8*
muscle fibres, fast and slow twitch,
  171–2
muscles
    cramp, *175–7*
    food for, *114*
    soreness, *182–4*
    strength, *5–6*
    warming up, *68–9*
music, *25–6, 88*

nasal strips, *213*
neck, alignment, *67–8*
Nike+ iPod Sport Kit, *26–7*
nipples, soreness, *182*
nutrition, *see* food

off-road running, *52–3*
online logging, *60*
orthotics, *73*
osteoarthritis, *227–8*
osteoporosis, *5, 228–9*
oxygen, *4*

pace
    measuring, *23, 24, 32*
    optimum, *30–1*
partners, running, *88–93*
passive rest, *167*
pedometers, *22–3*
personal bests, *102*
personal trainers, *93*
pilates, *170–1*
places to run, *48–59*
plantar fasciitis, *196–9*
pollen, *214*
Pose method, *161–4*
post-run nutrition, *135–8*
posture, *67–71*
power-walking, *221–3*
pregnancy, *215–19*
programmes
    for 5-km runs, *235–9*
    for 10-km runs, *242–5*
    for beginners, *35–6*
    for half marathons, *250–3*
    higher intensity, *40*
    for intermediate runners, *40–1*
    for novices, *38*
    pre-run, *220–3*
progress, measuring, *100–1, 102–3*
pronation, *71–3*
protein, *112–13, 114–16*
psychological effects, *7–10*
pulse rate, *3–4, 25*

quadriceps, stretching, *77–8*

races
    entering, *262*
    vs. events, *233*
    preparation for, *262–5*
rain, *19–20*
reasons for running, *93–4*
record-keeping, *59–61*
recovery walking, *30, 34*
rehydration, *see* hydration
relaxin (hormone), *217*
respiration, *4*

rest, passive vs. active, *167–8*
rest days, *37–8*
road running, *50–1*
Romanov, Nicholas, *161*
routes, *48–59*
routine, *29–30*
    importance of, *99*
rowing, *169*
'runner's high', *8–9*
Runner's World, *232*
running clubs, *92–3*
running events, *see* events
running fitness, *32–3*
running partners, *88–93*

safety, *26*
sand, running on, *53–4*
scheduling runs, *45–8*
self-esteem, *10*
shin splints, *204–7*
shoes, *15–17, 72*
    checking for wear, *205*
shorts, *18*
shoulders
    pain, *180*
    relaxing, *68*
side stitch, *177–80*
sleep, *7*
slow twitch muscles, *171–2*
SMART goals, *101–7*
snacks, *122–3*
socks, *19*
soleus muscles, *75–6*
speed
    measuring, *32*
    optimum, *30–1*
speed repetitions, *149–50*
speed training, *148–52*
sports drinks, *128, 131–3*
    for cramp, *177*
sports massage, *184–6*
sprints, *148–52*
steady sessions, *146*
sticking points, *166–7*
stitch, *177–80*

stopping training, effects, *50*
strengthening exercises, *208–10*
stretching, *66–7*
    post-run, *74–83*
style of running, *17*
sunglasses, *21*
sunscreen, *20*
supination, *71–3*
supplements, *138–9*
swimming, *169*

Talk Test, *30–1*
technique, *160–6*
temperature, during pregnancy, *217–18*
tendons, injury, *202–4*
thighs, stretching, *76–8, 80–1*
thirst, *131*
    see also hydration
time constraints, *45–8*
time of day for running, *41–5*
tops, *18–19*
training shoes, *15–17, 72*
    checking for wear, *205*
treadmill running, *54–6, 152–3*
trots, *180–1*
trousers, *18*

vitamins, *116–17*
    supplements, *139*

walking, *see* recovery walking
'walking resting pulse', *25*
warming up, *65–71*
water, *see* fluids
water containers, *21*
weather, *19–20*
websites, *268–70*
weight
    excess, *219–24*
    in pregnancy, *215–16*
weight loss and calories, *125*
weight training, *169–70*

yoga, *170*